EDUCATION ON THE INTERNET

THE WORLDWIDE CLASSROOM
Access to People, Resources, and
Curricular Connections

1999–2000 Update

Peggy A. Ertmer
Carole Hruskocy
Denise M. Woods
Purdue University

Merrill,
an imprint of Prentice Hall
Upper Saddle River, New Jersey   Columbus, Ohio

Editor: Debra A. Stollenwerk
Production Editor: JoEllen Gohr
Cover designer: Diane C. Lorenzo
Cover art: ©Photodisk, Inc.
Production Manager: Pamela Bennett
Director of Marketing: Kevin Flanagan
Marketing Manager: Meghan Shepherd
Marketing Coordinator: Krista Groshong

Copyright © 2000 by Prentice-Hall, Inc.
Pearson Education
Upper Saddle River, New Jersey 07458

Earlier editions of this work were written by Andrew T. Stull (1997 version) and Randall J. Ryder (1998-99 version).

Printed in the United States of America

10 9 8 7 6 5 4 3 2 1

ISBN: 0-13-014361-8

TRADEMARK INFORMATION:
Netscape Navigator is a registered trademark of Netscape Communications Corporation. *Internet Explorer* is a registered trademark of Microsoft Corporation.

The authors and publisher of this manual have used their best efforts in preparing this book. The authors and publisher make no warranty of any kind, expressed or implied, with regard to these programs or the documentation contained in this book. The authors and publisher shall not be liable in any event for incidental or consequential damages in connection with, or arising out of, the furnishing, performance, or use of the programs described in this book.

CONTENTS

INTRODUCTION

Welcome to the *Education on the Internet: The WorldWide Classroom*, a quick and easy guide to using the Internet in your classroom. As you may have already discovered, there is a wealth of information available on the Internet. Access to this information can transform classrooms into WorldWide Classrooms, teeming with rich and abundant information resources. But these transformations don't occur just because schools are connected to the Internet. Rather, a WorldWide Classroom evolves as educators learn to integrate these resources into meaningful curriculum-based learning experiences. With this text as your guide, we expect that you, too, will begin the transformation process—using worldwide resources to create rich learning experiences for your students.

WHO SHOULD USE THIS GUIDE?

This guide is designed for both current and future teachers. Whether you are located in a public or private school, urban or rural setting, an elementary or secondary classroom, this guide will help you access the Internet in ways that meet the needs of you *and* your students. Without getting too technical, we'll help you understand just enough about how the Internet works so that you can find and use the resources that are available on the Web.

WHAT RESOURCES ARE WITHIN THIS GUIDE?

This guide provides ideas for using the Internet to meet both your professional and instructional needs. For example, you will learn how to:

- connect with experts in your field
- join educational listservs
- participate in teacher chats
- conduct effective Internet searches
- create your own Web pages, and
- locate Web sites that are relevant to specific content needs

All of these topics address your professional needs. In addition, you will learn how to use these same Internet tools to create instructional activities that enable your students to:

- interact with experts

- collaborate with other students and teachers around the world
- participate in local and global projects
- publish original work
- evaluate the accuracy, credibility, and relevancy of Web site information

By addressing your professional *and* instructional needs in this book, we provide the tools you need to keep your own skills honed while simultaneously bringing your students up-to-speed.

HOW IS THIS GUIDE ORGANIZED?

If we had to describe the Internet in one word, that word would be *access*. We believe that the true power of the Internet lies in the access it provides to people, resources, and ideas. This is why we have organized this text around this theme. Thus, each of the first three sections in this book deals with a particular type of access that the Internet affords, while the last section deals with issues related to having Internet access.

There are a variety of Internet services available, each serving a different educational purpose. In this guide, we look, specifically, at using the Internet:

- as a communication tool
- as a tutoring/mentoring tool
- as a teaching/learning resource, and
- as a publishing house.

The first two applications connect us to *people*. The second two connect us to *resources*. These four applications, then, link us to two of the most important resources on the Internet.

In addition, the Internet has become a gold mine of teaching ideas, strategies, and lesson plans. Section 3 of this guide helps you access ideas that will help you to integrate the Internet into your curriculum in meaningful ways.

Finally, in the last section of this guide, we address issues related to Internet access: equity, safety, and responsibility. As with many valuable resources, the Internet is not completely risk-free. Both students and teachers need to be aware of potential problems and to practice thoughtful and responsible use.

2

NOTE: Readers should be aware that, due to the changing nature of the Internet, the sites listed in this text may have moved or changed by the time of publication!

WHAT IS THE INTERNET AND HOW MUCH DO I NEED TO KNOW ABOUT IT?

Although it is probably beneficial to know a little bit about the history of the Internet (it began 25 years ago), and to be able to define it (a combination, or network, of computers linked together), this information doesn't go very far to support your teaching or your students' learning. We believe that the most important thing you need to know about the Internet is *how to use it*! And along with that, you need to know how to help your students use it as a tool to achieve meaningful outcomes.

WHAT KINDS OF INTERNET USES ARE EMPHASIZED?

Like many others, we believe that the primary goal of education is to engage students in meaningful learning. According to Jonassen, Peck, and Wilson (1999), this includes helping students:

- recognize and solve problems
- comprehend new phenomena
- construct mental models of those phenomena
- set goals and regulate their own learning within each learning situation (p. 7)

Although the Internet can be used for lots of other reasons, this guide stresses using the Internet in ways that will facilitate students' accomplishment of the four goals listed above.

Together, the Internet and the World Wide Web have the potential to change the way we teach and learn. Yet the potential lies not in the amount of information that we can access, but in the way in which both teachers and students *interact* with that information. If we use the Internet primarily as an information resource (much like a library), then we will have left much of its potential untapped. For it is through the Internet's interactive capability that we are able to extend and transform the intellectual activity in our classrooms. The Internet makes it both possible and exciting to interact with others, with oral and visual information, and with scientific data. Because of this interactivity, our intellectual world can extend far beyond the traditional classroom walls.

Jonassen et al. (1999) noted that, "The Internet can immerse students in stimulating, challenging, motivating, and vibrant learning environments that provide a context in which computer literacy develops—not as a goal, but as a requirement in order to achieve much higher goals" (p. 20). These higher level goals relate to the skills and qualities that will be expected of all students in the future: creative thinking, problem solving, cooperation, independence, and·self-discipline, to name a few. In this book, we will help you think about how to facilitate these engaging types of uses, as well as point you to relevant Web sites that will get you started.

SUMMARY

The great news about the Internet is that it provides you with almost limitless amounts of up-to-date information. The bad news is that it provides you with almost limitless amounts of up-to-date information. Teachers are too busy to sort through all this information in order to find the perfect site for tomorrow's science lesson. This guide helps you sort through and manage that information so that you can locate and implement powerful lessons for your students today. Whether you teach in a kindergarten classroom or a high school chemistry classroom, this guide will serve as an excellent resource for both you and your students.

We hope that you enjoy your journey!

REFERENCES

Jonassen, D. H., Peck, K. L., & Wilson, B. G. (1999). *Learning with technology: A constructivist perspective.* Upper Saddle River, NJ: Merrill/ Prentice Hall.

SECTION 1: ACCESS TO PEOPLE

The Internet and World Wide Web open up numerous channels of communication for both teachers and students. Once connected, the possibilities for sending and receiving information across the Internet are many. Communication is enhanced through the use of the Internet as

- colleagues communicate with colleagues
- professionals from around the world share ideas
- teachers communicate with their students, and
- students converse with diverse populations around the world.

This section is organized into two parts. The first part introduces common ways to send and receive messages via the Internet including:

- email
- listservs
- mailing lists
- discussion groups
- chats
- bulletin boards
- newsgroups
- forums

The second part introduces the use of the Web for tutoring or mentoring. There are several Web sites that connect the user to "experts" who may provide help by answering questions or assisting on a project. These Web sites are commonly called:

- telementoring
- ask an expert

Teachers and students can benefit from the variety of communication channels made available through the Web. An abundance of information and ready resources are available with one click of the mouse. Classrooms can be transformed as teachers and students establish worldwide connections.

WHAT IS EMAIL?

"Email" stands for electronic mail. With email, a letter or message is sent from one person to another but without the help of the post office; instead, the written message is sent across the phone lines, from one computer to another. Without even picking up the phone your email message is sent to the intended receiver.

Both sender and receiver benefit from the convenience and ease of electronic mail. Email has become a common mode of communication because messages can be:

- immediately sent and received anywhere in the world
- delivered to any number of people at once
- sent according to the sender's time schedule
- delivered even if the receiver's phone line is busy
- accessed according to the receiver's schedule

Although email has quickly become a popular form of communication, users should proceed with caution. Your email remarks are not truly private. Email can be read by systems administrators or your email provider. Messages that you privately send can be forwarded (and edited) to/by others without your knowledge or permission.

WHAT DOES AN EMAIL ADDRESS LOOK LIKE?

An email address consists of four main parts:
- the user ID
- the "at" sign
- the domain name
- an extension

For example, an email address might look like this:

johndoe@mabell.gov

- the user ID = johndoe
- the "at" sign = @
- the domain name = mabell
- the extension = gov

The user ID is often the user's name. The "at" sign (@) always precedes the domain name. The domain name is the Internet server that houses the person's email account or the organization that provides your account (and for which you typically pay a monthly fee). The domain name is usually followed by the extension that signifies the type of organization sponsoring the account. Common extensions include *edu* for educational organizations, *gov* for government accounts, *com* for commercial organizations, and *net* for network providers.

To access your email account you will use a personal password. Together, you and your service provider will set up your email account and password. Some tips for protecting your account and insuring the confidentiality of your password include:

- use an uncommon password (avoid using your name, birthdate, etc.)
- use a combination of numbers and letters
- change your password often

HOW CAN I USE EMAIL FOR PROFESSIONAL PURPOSES?

Email offers many conveniences and saves time and energy. Messages to colleagues in the same building or school district can be sent and received right from your desk, including:

- reminders of meetings
- questions about needed resources
- messages concerning students or parents
- notes on school events

Once connected to the Internet you can email teachers outside of the school system. A vast array of resources are now at your fingertips as you begin communicating with a variety of teachers on educational issues such as lesson planning, classroom management, and technology implementation.

Besides traditional email, many Internet web sites can connect you to resources that may lead to email communications with online experts and classrooms around the world. Both you and your students can benefit from the following connections.

AskERIC
askeric@askeric.org

AskERIC is an Internet-based service that provides educational information to teachers, librarians, counselors, administrators, and parents, throughout the United States and around the world. It began as a project of the ERIC Clearinghouse on Information & Technology at Syracuse University. It contains the resources of the entire ERIC system and has a service in which you can ask educational questions of a staff of researchers.

Teacher-2-Teacher
http://www.teachnet.com/t2t/

Teacher-2-Teacher (T2T) mailing list connects you with 1500 teachers worldwide. This list focuses on the exchange of ideas relevant to preK–12 classrooms. Professional conversations and the sharing of lesson plans and teaching tips are part of the wide range of discussions at this site.

HOW CAN I USE EMAIL FOR INSTRUCTIONAL PURPOSES?

The Internet allows you to connect students with other students around the world. By connecting with other classrooms, unique projects or programs can be developed to:

- enhance the curriculum
- establish new friendships and
- enrich student communication skills

Some suggested activities to get you and your students connected around the world include:

- researching another classroom's city, state, or country
- collecting and sharing data on a common curriculum project
- establishing a database of contacts around the world
- collaborating on story writing
- exchanging pictures of local landmarks and historical figures
- sharing journal entries noting similarities and differences
- linking older and younger students via mentoring experiences

Visit the following addresses to find schools connected to the Internet.

Web Communities - International Friends
http://communities.msn.com/internationalfriends/

This Web site provides a list of newsgroups around the world. These community newsgroups are good places for discussing educational methods, experiences, and issues—and for asking or giving help. This site offers links to international friends from such countries as Africa, the Middle East, Europe, and South America. It also includes a link to monthly chats on various topics.

E-Mail Key Pal Connection http://www.comenius.com/keypal/index.html

This site offers registration for email key pals via a request form. Once registered, teachers and students can communicate electronically with other classrooms around the world.

BESIDES EMAIL, HOW CAN I COMMUNICATE THROUGH THE INTERNET?

Besides the basic, personal email message between two people there are various other techniques that allow for electronic communication between individuals or groups. These techniques have an assortment of names that may vary according to the resource that you consult. The most common names include:

- listservs
- mailing lists
- discussion groups
- chats
- bulletin boards
- newsgroups
- forums

Mailing lists and discussion group messages are emailed to individual subscribers. They are often referred to as listservs. Newsgroups and forums are messages posted on an electronic bulletin board for anyone to read and answer. They may also be called bulletin boards or "BBS" (bulletin board service).

These terms are often interchanged by authors and Internet users. Thus, for the average Internet user, understanding the technical differences between these terms is often confusing. The important thing to know is that listservs, mailing lists, discussion groups, chats, newsgroups, bulletin boards, and forums are all types of electronic communication that connect you with a variety of people and resources around the world.

WHAT ARE MAILING LISTS AND DISCUSSION GROUPS?

A *mailing list* allows an individual to send email to multiple recipients at the same time. A mailing list requires the user to subscribe in order to send and receive such messages. The first subscription mailing list administered by a computer was a program called LISTSERV; thus, "mailing list" and "listserv" are often used synonymously.

When using a mailing list you first send email to the designated mailing list address. The message is then automatically copied and sent to all other members who have subscribed to the mail list. This method is especially useful when sharing information with a group and can be done through either a private or public listserv. Private listservs restrict membership to certain groups such as people working together on committees or a group of college classmates.

Both mailing lists and discussion groups may be referred to as listservs, but they differ slightly. With mailing lists, often a single person produces messages for distribution to subscribers. In contrast, *discussion groups* resemble conversation between many people on a common topic of interest. Anyone can contribute a message that all subscribers will receive. Some discussion groups are open; some require membership. Users participate in discussion groups with the specific intent of requesting or offering information about a set topic.

Discussion groups are often affiliated with academic organizations. Teachers may connect to discussion groups based on individual interests or geographical regions such as special education, science, language arts, or the Midwest. Discussion groups can provide valuable links to professional colleagues around the world.

Both mailing lists and discussion groups offer asynchronous communication, that is, the sender leaves a message to be read at the receiver's convenience. Synchronous communication, where the sender and receiver participate in a real time conversation, is also possible through the Internet. This form of communication allows the sender and receiver to "chat" in real time and is commonly referred to as a "chat channel" or "chat room."

The following Web site can connect you with several chat channels.

Kidlink
http://www.kidlink.org/

Kidlink offers a private network of real time interactions or "chats" for both teachers and students. At this site, participants can link with people from a variety of countries for conversation and sharing. Online activities are also available in many different languages. Student participation is limited to people age 15 and younger.

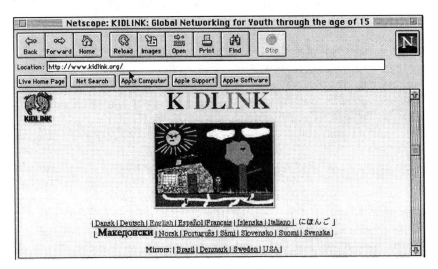

Copyright (1998) by Kidlink Society. Reprinted with permission.

HOW DO I SUBSCRIBE TO A LISTSERV?

Sign-up procedures for each listserv will vary, but generally you send an email message to the address of the list manager. The procedure is simple and requires little time. A typical subscribe message is typed in the body of the email text and looks like:

Subscribe listname firstname lastname

An example might be

Subscribe EDCI564 carole hruskocy

This message assures that Carole Hruskocy is signed onto the EDCI 564 class mailing list and can communicate with her students by using one common email address.

Typically listservs follow these procedures for subscribing:

- email your message to the listserv address
- leave the subject line blank
- write the subscribe message in the body of the email
- remove any "signature blocks" at the end of your email

Most listservs send you a message confirming your membership. Once you are registered, you will receive many messages from other listserv members. Just remember that any message you send to the list will be viewed by all members of that listserv. You have the option to unsubscribe at any point in time. Instructions are usually provided in the original confirmation message.

WHAT ARE NEWSGROUPS AND FORUMS?

This type of electronic communication differs from the traditional mailing list and discussion group listserv because messages are not delivered to your personal electronic mailbox. Users must visit a particular Web site to read others' messages and post their own.

Newsgroups and forums offer additional ways of collaborating on the Internet. Like listservs, they provide an arena for sharing similar interests or discussing related topics. Global communication is enhanced as users share their thoughts and ideas on subjects of mutual interest and concern.

Unlike listservs, newsgroup and forum participants do not have to sign up or subscribe. Messages are posted on an electronic bulletin board. Individuals may visit the bulletin board to look for messages of interest and to post replies. Your reply will show up on the bulletin board thus broadcasting your words for all to see. Anyone can search the Web and join in these discussions.

Because these bulletin boards are accessible to every Internet user the level of discussion can vary from highly intellectual to unenlightened. Some newsgroups and forums are moderated for content but discussion is usually uncensored. Users may be exposed to a wide variety of beliefs, which may differ radically from their own. Participants should be aware of the open nature of newsgroup and forum conversations and proceed with caution.

HOW CAN I USE ELECTRONIC COMMUNICATION
FOR PROFESSIONAL PURPOSES?

Listservs and bulletin boards can connect you to professionals around the world. By subscribing to a listserv you'll be able to participate in professional discussions on a variety of topics such as those listed below. By connecting to a bulletin board you'll access a variety of thoughts on a selected topic and may add your own ideas as well. Common themes include:

- national and state curricular standards
- curricular requirements and activities
- discipline techniques
- classroom management
- technology integration
- professional development
- restructuring and school change

Several listservers, specific to the use of the Internet and educational technology, are provided below. Email addresses and instructions for subscribing to the listserv are also included.

EDTECH
This discussion list centers on issues related to educational technology. To subscribe, address an email message in the following manner:

(send the message to)
listserv@msu.edu
(in the body of the message type)
Subscribe EDTECH firstname lastname

WEBTALK
This list promotes discussion on integrating the World Wide Web into curricula. To subscribe, address an email message in the following manner:

(send the message to)
majordomo@teachers.net
(in the body of the message type)
Subscribe WEBTALK your email address

IDEAS_LIST

Collaborative Learning Project Ideas List
This list offers information on a number of mailing lists. To obtain a list of publicly available mailing lists on this system:

(send the message to)
majordomo@gsn.org
(in the body of the message type)
lists

Each line will contain the name of a mailing list and a brief description of the list. To get more information about a particular list, use the "info" command, supplying the name of the list. For example, if the name of the list for which you wish information is "demo-list," you would type in the body of the mail message

info demo-list

WWWEDU

This is the Internet's largest forum on the use of the World Wide Web in education. *WWWEDU* is a moderated discussion with over 1600 members from 35 countries. To subscribe, address an email message in the following manner:

(send the message to)
listproc@ready.cpb.org
(in the body of the message type)
Subscribe WWWEDU firstname lastname

Because there is a vast array of mailing lists, discussion groups, newsgroups, and forums available on the Internet, locating appropriate groups may be difficult and time consuming. There are a number of Web sites that simplify this process by providing indexes of available listservs. These addresses might be a good place to start your search for online professional discussions.

Liszt

http://www.liszt.com/

This is a directory of email discussion groups. *Liszt* allows you to search over 71,000 mailing lists by keyword or topic.

Reference.com

http://www.reference.com/

This Web site offers another way to locate newsgroups, discussion groups, and forums. The user types in a keyword in the search box and receives a list of relevant newsgroup postings. One unique feature of this service is a user profile system that allows you to store questions at *Reference.com* for periodic email updates.

TILE.NET/LISTS

http://tile.net/lists/

Tile.net is an index of mailing lists grouped by topic. This site serves as a quick reference to a variety of Internet discussion and information lists.

Deja News

http://dejanews.com/

This site provides a useful tool for exploring hundreds of newsgroups. You can search the archive of Usenet postings by keyword, author, and date. The archive is updated every two days.

Forum One

http://forumone.com/

Forum One is a searchable directory of more than 48,000 message boards from sites around the Web. You can type a keyword in the search box and receive a list of topics that will link you to specific forums on the Web.

tech.Learning

http://www.techlearning.com

This site includes a link to the *Well Connected Educator*. Click on this link to access information about forums for sharing success stories, models, strategies, and specific examples of how to use technology for teaching and learning. This site also provides a publishing center for students' work.

Voices of Youth Website
http://www.unicef.org/voy/index.html

Sponsored by the United Nations Children Fund (UNICEF), this Web site offers three forums. Teachers and students can express views on current global issues, participate in interactive global learning projects, or discuss and exchange experiences about electronic networks or global educational projects.

Teachers Helping Teachers
http://www.pacificnet.net/~mandel/

This Web site is the home page by teachers, for teachers. *Teachers Helping Teachers* is an online network of teachers sharing ideas about classroom management, special education, and every subject area in the K–12 curriculum. A teacher chat occurs every week.

School.Net
http://www.k12.school.net/go/forums/

SchoolNet provides online discussion groups for teachers, students, parents, and others interested in education. Forums are organized by subject area, educational topics, and/or peer groups. Some educational groups have their own specific forums.

HOW CAN I USE ELECTRONIC COMMUNICATION FOR INSTRUCTIONAL PURPOSES?

With the help of the World Wide Web, students can interact with others outside of the local learning community on a daily basis. Listservs and bulletin boards can enhance the classroom curriculum and enrich students' learning experiences. Through these Internet exchanges students can:

- investigate topics of interest
- seek answers to research questions
- receive help on homework questions
- establish friendships with students around the world

KidsCom
http://kidscom.com/

This site offers twelve different activity areas that will be most appealing to younger kids. Within each area kids can ask questions about the Internet, post messages to a Graffiti Wall, find a pen pal, and follow the space adventures of Spec and Tra.

Homework Help
http://www.startribune.com/stonline/html/special/homework/

This Web site serves as a homework resource for elementary, junior high, or high school students. Students can get the help they need on their homework by posting questions to *The Minneapolis–St. Paul Star Tribune Homework Help* site. Questions are answered by teachers from around the country.

WHY ARE EMAIL, LISTSERVS, AND BULLETIN BOARDS USEFUL COMMUNICATION TOOLS?

Email is like leaving "voice mail" on someone's computer. It provides a fast, convenient method of communicating across distances. One of the chief benefits is the flexibility offered to senders and receivers of messages. As with voice mail, the receiver need not be present. The added advantage to email is that your message will be delivered even if the phone line is busy.

Mailing lists and bulletin boards simplify communication between individuals and groups. Whether connecting a teacher to a group of students or to a group of professionals sharing similar interests, mailing lists and bulletin boards provide multiple channels of communication in one convenient format.

WHAT IS TELEMENTORING?

Through the Internet you can tap into a whole new community of learners. Visiting someone's Web site may introduce you to many new ideas. Yet this experience represents only one way of learning from the Internet. Exchanging ideas and information is another, more active way to learn from the Internet and World Wide Web.

Traditional mentoring involves an exchange of information between an "expert" and a "novice." The expert/mentor is an experienced individual who gives guidance, support, and encouragement to the novice/mentee. An ongoing relationship is formed whereby each participant benefits from the experience. Mentors experience a feeling of fulfillment for having "made a difference" and having helped their partner succeed. Mentees receive individualized assistance on problems they encounter during the learning process. Often lasting friendships are formed.

Telementoring offers all the benefits of traditional mentoring as mentors and mentees are connected via email or the World Wide Web. The purpose of the mentoring may be to provide information on specific subjects or to provide guidance on life goals and decisions. Knowledgeable adults consult with students about their school work offering advice and critical feedback. Telementoring formats may include:

- one-to-one
- moderated group
- unmoderated group
- peer mentoring

Telementoring provides opportunities for formal and informal communication between students, teachers, and professionals in the outside world. These multiple mentoring experiences are available:

- parent-student
- inservice teacher–preservice teacher
- content expert-student
- college student–high school student
- teacher-teacher

HOW CAN I FIND OUT MORE ABOUT HOW TELEMENTORING WORKS?

One way to experience telementoring is by visiting a Web site that simulates the actual telementoring process. You can choose either to follow the progress of one student's telementoring experience or to participate in the experience yourself. Visit these sites to find out more about mentoring via the Internet.

Mentor Center
http://mentorcenter.bbn.com/

Find out how one fifth-grade English class uses the *Mentor Center* for help

18

with their written work. This site includes a "Take the Tour" link that demonstrates how one student and a mentor utilized their student/mentor connection.

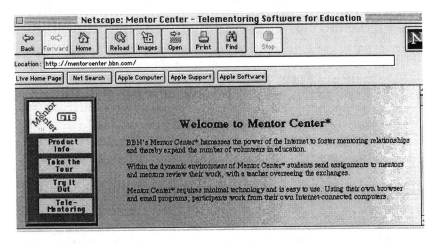

Copyright (1997) by BBN Corporation. Reprinted with permission.

Exploring the World of Telementoring
http://www.tapr.org/~ird/Wadbrook/telementoring/WebQuest.htm

This site offers a WebQuest journey that introduces users to the concept of telementoring. Telementoring benefits, limitations, and resources are included. Successful telementoring programs and suggested readings are also provided. (WebQuests are described in more detail in Section 3.)

*HOW CAN I USE TELEMENTORING FOR PROFESSIONAL
AND INSTRUCTIONAL PURPOSES?*

Telementoring offers unique opportunities for both teachers and students. Teachers can either serve as a mentor for other individuals or link with a mentor of their own. Students can connect with mentors to receive individual assistance and personalized feedback.

A few examples of how teachers can advance professional and instructional knowledge through telementoring include:

- serve as a mentor to a student
- sign up as a mentor to a new teacher
- connect with a mentor regarding educational technology
- link with a mentor in a specific curriculum area
- locate a mentor to help plan a new unit of study

Students can expand their knowledge and skills through telementoring by:

- receiving individual help on written assignments
- connecting with a mentor in a special area of interest
- getting feedback on homework
- linking with a mentor for research

Telementoring offers many advantages for teachers and students. Partnerships can be established to guide or reinforce learning. All participants in a telementoring alliance can benefit from this unique experience.

WHAT ARE SOME SUGGESTED TELEMENTORING SITES FOR PROFESSIONAL AND INSTRUCTIONAL USE?

Electronic Emissary
http://www.tapr.org/emissary/

This Web site will help link volunteer professionals with teachers and their classrooms. Teachers search the database of available experts, choose one, and request a match. The *Electronic Emissary* will help set up a mentor program, all carried out by email.

Tutor 2000
http://www.tutor2000.com/

Tutor 2000 is the first nationwide online tutoring referral service. Sponsored by the National Tutoring Association of America, this site allows tutors to advertise their professional expertise. Students can browse through tutor listings for an appropriate match.

HP Telementor Program
http://www.telementor.org/hp/info/resources.html

Visit this site to learn about Hewlett Packard's email mentor program. This site has an index of links to general program information and resources. It also provides links to K–12 resources, math/science interactive projects, and other mentoring programs.

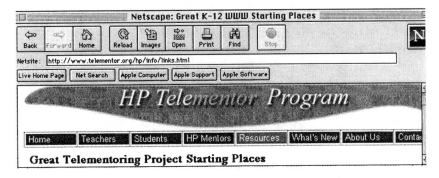

Center for Children & Technology (CCT) Telementoring Young Women in Science, Math, and Technology Project
http://www.edc.org/CCT/telementoring

This project is funded by the National Science Foundation. Female high school students are provided opportunities to get involved in an online mentoring relationship. Professional women in the field of science volunteer to serve as mentors, focusing on career guidance and personal development.

AT&T Learning Network—Ask LN
http://www.att.com/learningnetwork/whatln.html

Have a question about how to use technology in your classroom? This Web site offers guidance and advice on educational technology issues. A network of mentors, teachers with experience integrating technology into the K–12 classroom, provide coaching and information on how to use technology effectively.

WHAT IS "ASK AN EXPERT"?

Teachers and students often have questions for which answers may not be easily found in a textbook. The World Wide Web offers one means for expanding your search. Several Web sites present an array of qualified "experts" who can help answer your questions. These experts may be teachers or professionals in the area you are researching. You can post your question to the expert by email or by visiting the appropriate Web site. Answers are usually received in a few days or less.

HOW CAN I USE "ASK AN EXPERT" FOR PROFESSIONAL AND INSTRUCTIONAL PURPOSES?

Both teachers and students can benefit by visiting "ask an expert" Web sites. Valuable information resources are readily available each time you access these sites.

Teachers can use "ask an expert" to:

- find answers to curricular-specific questions
- acquire professional resources
- discover curricular connections
- investigate professional development opportunities

Students can use "ask an expert" to:

- extend research projects
- find homework help
- investigate past discoveries
- separate fact from fiction

Visit some of the following "ask an expert" sites or send an email message to those addresses listed below.

"Ask an Expert" Web sites

SchoolWorld
http://www.schoolworld.asn.au/

SchoolWorld is an exceptional site for educators. This site includes a Tek-Teachers link where "teacher experts" answer questions on a wide range of subjects. At this site teachers can sign onto a listserv connecting all *SchoolWorld* members. *SchoolWorld* also provides Internet programs and projects for you and your students to join.

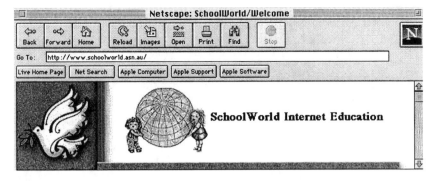

The Savvy Cyber Teacher
http://k12science.ati.stevens-tech.edu/cyberteacher/week2web.html

The *Savvy Cyber Teacher* includes a variety of tips for using the Internet effectively in the K–12 classroom. An index of links called "finding online experts," which will connect you with several "ask an expert" web pages, is also available. Users can access links to sample projects that use online experts at this Web site.

NASA's Quest Project
http://quest.arc.nasa.gov

This Web site connects you to NASA's space scientists and space team. This site also provides a directory of their online events and interactive projects. This NASA site is a great resource for students who hope to become future astronauts.

Ask Jeeves for Kids
http://www.ajkids.com/

Have a question about any topic? Why not ask Jeeves? This simple question and answer format serves as a great resource for students and teachers.

"Ask an Expert" email addresses

Ask a Geologist

Have a question about earthquakes, volcanoes, minerals, or rocks? Send an email message to the geology expert at

ask-a-geologist@usgs.gov

Jane Goodall Institute

Ever wonder how much an elephant eats in one day? Jane Goodall is an expert on animals from around the world. You might even ask Jane about her work with animals at the San Diego Zoo. Send an email message to:

jg@gsn.org

Scientist on Tap

While at this site you can ask a scientist about jet propulsion. This Web site describes various jet propulsion research projects conducted at California's

Jet Propulsion Laboratory. Scientists are available to answer questions from students and teachers at the following email address:

scientist-on-tap@gsn.org

SUMMARY

This section introduced a variety of ways to communicate across the Internet including the three most common forms—*email, listservs,* and *bulletin boards. Telementoring* and *Ask the Expert* were also introduced as additional resources for establishing communication across the Web.

In using the communication channels that the Web provides, teachers and students can benefit greatly by connecting to a vast number of people around the world. Communication and research skills can be enhanced, resulting in rich learning experiences for all. The classroom curriculum can be transformed as teaching and learning experiences extend beyond the existing school structure.

SECTION 2: ACCESS TO RESOURCES

The Web is a wonderful educational resource. Both teachers and students can use the Web to search for information on a variety of topics. A teacher can access thousands of lesson plans, categorized by grade level or subject matter. A student can access books in a library that is half way around the world. In addition, there are numerous sites dedicated to educational research and funding opportunities. Finally, the Web provides teachers with an effective resource for professional development. In this section we discuss these four main uses of the Web:

- information source
- research tool
- lesson plan bank
- professional development tool

HOW CAN I USE THE WEB AS AN INFORMATION SOURCE?

The Web is one of the foremost sources of information in this century. Students and teachers can easily visit Web sites that contain information on a wide variety of topics.

Web documents, graphics, and audio and video clips all contribute to the learning experience. With a point and a click, students have access to government sites, museums, and libraries. Teachers have access to these resources as well as lesson plans and professional development tutorials.

WHAT ARE SEARCH ENGINES?

The most efficient way to find information on the Web is to use a search engine. Search engines are programs that categorize information in databases and then retrieve that information in the form of searches. Search engines provide two levels of search options. First, most search engines categorize information into a table of contents. The user can look for information by clicking the links within the search engine's categorized index.

Search engines also use electronic robots, together with indexing software, to look through new Web pages, searching for keywords within those pages. The keywords are stored in a database of information. This allows you to utilize another type of search by entering keywords associated with the topic on which you want information. The search engine database compares your search statement to the information in its database. It then returns a list of Web pages that contain the keywords that you have entered.

For example, a search for the words "Lesson Plans" would return a number of different Web sites that contain the words "Lesson Plans" somewhere on the page. The user would then visit one of the Web sites listed by clicking on the link.

HOW CAN I CONDUCT AN EFFECTIVE SEARCH?

Search engines use Boolean logic to compare keywords. Boolean logic can help limit your search through the use of AND, OR, and NOT in your keyword statement. As an example, a user can search for math AND elementary or math NOT secondary. A few tips for conducting an effective search include:

- The keywords that you use in your search should neither be too narrow nor too broad. For example, the word "education" is far too broad, but searching on the keywords "education AND fourth AND grade AND math NOT metrics" may be too narrow.
- If you get too many "hits" from a search, narrow it down using Boolean operators.
- Use the Advanced Search features that most engines have, such as limiting your search to Web sites or to Images on the Web.
- Use more than one search engine to gather information; each engine has its own database, so search results will be different.
- Use search engines that search more than one search engine at a time, thus saving you time.

There are many different search engines on the Web. Some of the more popular ones are:

Lycos
http://www.lycos.com

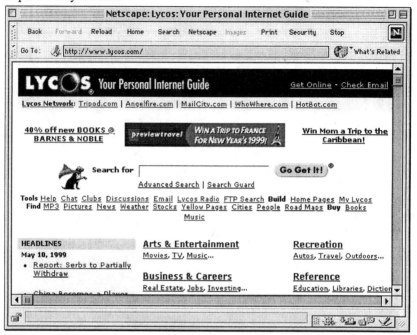

Copyright (1998) by Lycos, Inc. Lycos is a registered trademark of Carnegie Mellon University. All rights reserved. Reprinted with permission.

Yahoo
http://www.yahoo.com

Alta Vista
http://altavista.digital.com

Infoseek
http://guide.infoseek.com

Excite
http://excite.com

A search engine designed specifically for students is:

28

Yahooligans
http://www.yahooligans.com

Web sites that search multiple search engines simultaneously include:

All-in-One Search
http://wcross.iserver.net/

Internet Sleuth
http://www.isleuth.com

Inference Find
http://www.infind.com

Dogpile
http://www.dogpile.com/

HOW CAN I USE THE WEB AS A RESEARCH TOOL?

Initially, the primary users of the Internet were researchers at universities and
governmental organizations. In the early 1990s, businesses realized that the
Internet was a valuable tool for advertising their unique products or services
and keeping track of the competition. Today, educational institutions are one
of the fastest growing groups accessing information on the Internet.

There are many ways to use the Internet for research, including:
- exploring libraries to search for information
- locating articles and other documents related to your research topic
- visiting Web sites directly related to your topic (e.g., animals,
  science)

There are many sites dedicated to educational research on the Web including:

United States Department of Education
http://www.ed.gov

The *U.S. Department of Education* includes links to the latest educational
headlines, funding opportunities, student financial assistance, research and
statistics, news and events, as well as a directory to other educational
resources.

Library Catalogs
http://library.ncsu.edu/

This site provides a list of library catalogs, including the North Carolina State University library, U.S. government libraries, and Triangle Research Libraries Network (TRLN). Library servers on the WWW (from the Berkeley Digital Library Sunsite) and Library catalogs on the WWW (from University of Saskatchewan Libraries) are also available.

American Library Association
http://www.ala.org

The *American Library Association* provides leadership for the development, promotion, and improvement of library and information services and the profession of librarianship to enhance learning and ensure access to information for all.

Library of Congress
http://www.loc.gov

The mission of the *Library of Congress* is to make its resources available to Congress and the American people. The *Library of Congress* attempts to sustain and preserve a collection of knowledge and creativity for future generations. Access to the *Library of Congress* also includes links to services provided for researchers and K-12 educators.

The Internet Public Library
http://ipl.sils.umich.edu

The *Internet Public Library* (IPL) is the first public library of the Internet. *IPL* is committed to providing library services to the Internet community, to learn and teach what librarians have to contribute in a digital environment, to promote librarianship and the importance of libraries, and to share interesting ideas and techniques with other librarians.

Peterson's Education Center
http://www.petersons.com/ugrad

This Web site brings together, at one central address, consistently organized information about educational opportunities at all levels, and gives individuals the ability to search Peterson's databases. In addition, users can request more information and interact in other ways with faculty and administrators at educational institutions.

Developing Educational Standards
http://putwest.boces.org/Standards.html

Successful lesson plans have clear goals based on educational standards. This Web site has an index to sources of information on educational standards and curricular frameworks from all sources (national, state, and local).

Educational Technology (Edutech)
http://tecfa.unige.ch/info-edu-comp.html

Educational Technology is an online resource for education and technologies. It offers a variety of options including sites of the month, an alphabetical search for themes, a query search, and an opportunity to submit a theme to Edutech's database.

JASON Project
http://www.jasonproject.org/

JASON Project is a year-round scientific expedition designed to excite and engage students in science and technology and to motivate and provide professional development for teachers. The *JASON Project* has been considered a leader in distance learning programs, which is continually expanding by adding more "components" to the Project experience.

Global School Network
http://www.gsn.org/
The Global SchoolNet Foundation (GSN) is a major contributor to Internet-based learning. GSN offers a variety of free support services to learners and provides the help needed to get started. GSN collaborates with individuals, schools, businesses and community organizations to

design, develop, and manage hundreds of collaborative projects each
year.

Copyright (1999) by GSN. Reprinted with permission.

Learning Research and Development Center (LRDC)
http://alan.ldrc.pitt.edu/lrdc/

LRDC has a twofold mission: to broaden scientific insights into all aspects of
learning and to support the use of research in instructional settings, including
classrooms, industry and museums.

Virtual Schoolhouse Educational Resources
http://metalab.unc.edu/cisco/schoolhouse/lounge/subjects/

This Web site contains links to a variety of resources, categorized by subject
matter including English, math, foreign languages, physical education,
history, and sciences.

One of the main reasons the Web has gained the attention of educational institutions is the wide variety of lesson plans and activities available. Many teachers are creating Web pages that describe successful plans or activities. These are often categorized by grade level or subject matter. Many Web sites also include student and teacher ratings of lesson plans. Some Web resources for locating lesson plans and curriculum activities include:

CEARCH: The Cisco Educational Archive
http://sunsite.unc.edu:80/cisco/web-arch.html

CEARCH is a resource for teachers or schools interested in finding out more about the Internet. It provides information on how to use the Internet in the classroom, and how a school can get wired.

Heinemann Interactive
http://www.heinemann.com.au/index.html

Heinemann Interactive contains online resources for classroom use, online catalogs and ordering, and the latest educational news.

Education Resource List
http://www.dpi.state.wi.us/dpi/dlcl/lbstat/ed_res.html

This listing includes over 400 sites divided into subject or curricular areas. General sites are listed first in each section, followed by sites related to specific subject areas or to K–12 education.

Sendit K–12 Resources
http://www.sendit.nodak.edu/sendit/teacher.html

Sendit K–12 Resources links to a multitude of resources for teachers, including lesson plans, tutorials and workshops. Information is categorized by subject matter.

Indiana University Bookstore
http://www.indiana.edu/~eric_rec/bks/lessons.html

This site contains free lesson plans together with the capability to search by topic for resources and alphabetical listings of publications.

The World-Wide Web Virtual Library: Education
http://www.csu.edu.au/education/library.html

You can search the *Education Virtual Library* at this Web site. Libraries are listed alphabetically by site, education level, resources provided, type of site, and country.

Collaborative Lesson Archive
http://faldo.atmos.uiuc.edu/CLA/

The *Collaborative Lesson Archive* (CLA) is intended to be a forum for the creation, distribution, and archival of education curricula for all grade levels and subject areas. CLA provides the framework and the storage area; the quantity and quality of the content is entirely dependent on the Internet community.

Education World
http://www.education-world.com

This Web site is a valuable online resource that helps simplify the education community's use of the Internet. *Education World* is designed to help educators with lesson planning and classroom projects as well as in their own continuing educational and professional development. It features an education-specific search engine with links to over 100,000 sites. *Education World* offers monthly reviews of other educational Web sites, grade-specific search engines, national education employment listings, curricular tools, lesson plans, forums, news, and other weekly original content.

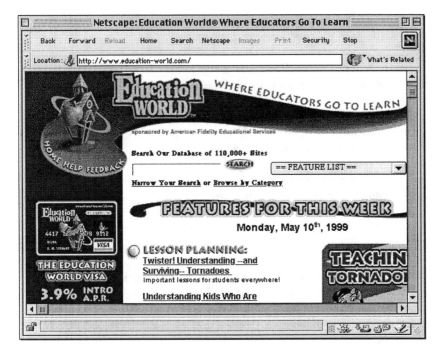

New York Times Learning Network
http://www.nytimes.com/learning/

The *New York Times* Web site is a storehouse of educational information. It contains current news articles rewritten for students in grades 6–12. It is loaded with lesson plans, activities, a crossword puzzle for kids, connections to this day in history, the latest educational news, and more.

The Digital Classroom
http://www.nara.gov/education/teaching/teaching.html

This Web site contains reproducible primary documents, lesson plans correlated to the National History Standards, and cross-curricular connections.

AskERIC Lesson Plan Collection
http://ericir.syr.edu/Virtual/Lessons/

The *AskERIC* Lesson Plan Collection contains more than 1000 unique lesson plans which have been written and submitted by teachers from all over the United States.

Apple Computers
http://henson.austin.apple.com/edres/lessonmenu.shtml

The *Apple Computers* site contains lesson plans by teachers for teachers, divided into elementary, middle, and high school levels.

Crayola Art Education
http://education.crayola.com/lessons/

This site has lesson plans that utilize crayons, pencils, markers, paint, and modeling compounds. The plans help students to recognize that creative communication involves not only language and visual arts but also social studies, science, and math.

HOW CAN I USE THE WEB FOR PROFESSIONAL DEVELOPMENT?

Professional development has never been easier than it is on the Internet. Tutorials, online forums and courses, and pages of text resources are available to help educators learn more about technology and its use in the classroom. Distance education is becoming more of a reality because of the supporting technologies and the proliferation of information. Some professional development Web sites include:

Apple Education—Staff Development
http://www.eworld.com/education/k12/staffdev/

Simply putting computers in classrooms does not guarantee a positive change in the teaching and learning process. The success of technology in schools depends on the skills of the teacher. This Web site provides a staff development forum that helps teachers reach the point where they're using technology tools with the same ease with which they use books, maps, pencils, and pens.

Teacher/Pathfinder Professional Development
http://teacherpathfinder.org/ProfDev/professional.html

A multitude of links to preservice, inservice, continuing education, professional organizations, and tutorials is available on this site.

The Virtual Schoolhouse Career Development
http://metalab.unc.edu/cisco/schoolhouse/lounge/career.html

The *Virtual Schoolhouse Career Development* Web site contains links to professional development sites. Links include sites at which you can take courses via the Internet, find out about educational conferences, and read the latest publications. In addition, other links contain a plethora of well-researched educational resources and information.

Pathways to School Improvement
http://www.ncrel.org/ncrel/sdrs/areas/pd0cont.htm

Pathways was designed to support teams engaged in the School Improvement Cycle. Teachers, parents, and students can browse the 18 topic areas to see a listing of critical issues available or under development. Additional full-text material, links to other related Internet sites, and a number of other resources are also available.

Critical Thinking for Primary and Secondary
http://www.sonoma.edu/cthink/K12/

The trend toward an emphasis on developing critical thinking skills is one of the most significant changes in educational philosophy in the latter half of this century. This Web site provides background articles, dialogue forums, guidelines, and lessons to help incorporate critical thinking into the curriculum.

Educational Technology Training Center (ETTC) for Middlesex County, NJ
http://www.techtrain.org/

ETTC is a comprehensive resource for educators in Middlesex County, New Jersey, and throughout the world. The site includes technology integration workshops, lesson plans, links to Internet resources, tips on teaching in a one-computer classroom, and more.

Apple Virtual Campus

http://www.apple.com/education/k12/events/semseries/

The *Apple Virtual Campus* contains a series of virtual seminars that show how schools successfully implement technology, how they choose digital content, and how they integrate technology into the curriculum.

Copyright (1999) by Apple Computer, Inc. Reprinted with permission.

World School Program

http://www.bell-atl.com/wschool

The *World School Program* is a private non-profit organization that promotes business and community involvement in public schools. Grants, awards, training, and development are all available. The site is used to recruit community and business volunteers to support public schools and conduct research and analysis of critical education issues.

The Well

http://www.well.com

The *WELL* is an online gathering place. *WELL* members engage in discussion, swap information, express their convictions and greet their friends in online forums known as conferences.

From Now On: The Educational Technology Journal

http://fromnowon.org/

This Web site provides a variety of professional development tools. Articles on many educational topics are available, including those on Internet policies, staff development, research, and parenting.

PC Magazine on the Web

http://www.zdnet.com/pcmag

You can find out about the latest technology hardware and software at this site as well as information about how to use it.

Scholastic Magazine

http://scholastic.com

Children's books, book fairs, curriculum programs, and classroom materials are all available at this Web site. *Scholastic Magazine* is a global children's publishing and media company in both education and entertainment. Scholastic's reputation for quality, learning, and fun is based on a long-term relationship with teachers, parents, and children, and its unique ability to understand what kids want and need for their education and entertainment.

Engines for Education

http://www.ils.nwu.edu/~e_for_e/nodes/I-M-INTRO-ZOOMER-pg.html

This Web site has a series of questions and answers to some of the most important educational issues today.

c/net

http://www.cnet.com/

Learn about computer hardware, software, and gadgets at *c/net*. The latest technology is discussed at a level that is understandable. Web authoring topics also are discussed. This Web site also provides access to downloads of new technology software.

Inter-Links Internet Access
http://alabanza.com/kabacoff/Inter-Links/

Inter-Links is an Internet navigator, resource locator, and tutorial. It is designed to help you navigate the Internet and find useful resources quickly and efficiently.

Quest: NASA K–12 Internet Initiative
http://quest.arc.nasa.gov

The mission of *Quest: NASA K–12 Internet Initiative* is to provide support and services for schools, teachers, and students to fully utilize the Internet and its underlying information technologies. Information is available on how to bring the Internet into your classroom with a comprehensive look at Internet science.

Netscape Netcenter What's Cool Page
http://home.mcom.com/home/whats-cool.html

Find out about the latest ideas in technology through this Web site. Learn about what makes Web sites work and how technology can be used in the classroom.

SUMMARY

The teaching/learning opportunities on the Internet are endless. Teachers, students, administrators, and parents can all find valuable information and resources by conducting effective searches. Educational institutions are just beginning to scratch the surface of the Internet. The future promises to hold many more opportunities.

So far in this text, we have concentrated on *getting* information from the Internet. The Internet would not be what it is today, however, without people *putting* information on the Internet also. There are numerous Web sites with information on setting up Web sites in your school and publishing your own Web pages. What better resource could there be *about* the Web than one that you find *on* the Web?

Like print media, Web pages have one main purpose: to convey information. In an educational setting, a Web page can be used:

- to convey background information about the school
- as a notification board for parents regarding meeting times, important dates, days off, lunch menu
- to display curriculum, lesson plans, teachers' biographies
- to publish student work

What are Web pages, Web sites, and Web servers?

There are many terms that are important to understand before discussing Web page development.

- A *Web page* is a document that you view in your browser (e.g., Internet Explorer, Netscape). The document can fill one screen or multiple screens, giving the user the ability to scroll down to view it all.
- A *Web site* is a group of Web pages that are created and maintained by a group or individual.
- A *Web server* is a computer that runs software that allows Web pages to be "served" or shown via a browser. The information stored on a Web server is available to anyone with access to the Internet.
- A Web page is *published* (or uploaded to a Web server) by using the publishing feature provided in the authoring tools or using File Transfer Protocol (FTP) software.

Creating a Web page can be a valuable and fun exercise for both teachers and students. Many school systems have extensive Web sites that list valuable information about their use of technology.

There are two main ways to create your own Web page:
- use a Web authoring tool
- use a programming language

These techniques are discussed in the following sections.

Using a Web authoring tool is a great idea for those who do not want to become programmers. Authoring tools are sophisticated software packages that provide an easy way to create Web pages. Templates and themes are available in most of these products that allow the user to create entire Web sites. The following Web authoring programs are easy to use and provide a number of powerful and useful functions. Each product can be downloaded from the URL listed, for a 30-day free trial.

Microsoft FrontPage
http://www.microsoft.com

Adobe Systems PageMill
http://www.adobe.com

Web Wizard
http://www.halcyon.com/artamedia/webwizard

NetObjects Fusion
http://www.netobjects.com

HOW CAN I USE HYPERTEXT MARKUP LANGUAGE (HTML)?

Hypertext Markup language (HTML) is the simplest, most commonly used programming language of the Web. HTML has become a popular choice for Web development because it is platform independent, allowing Web pages to be viewed on any type of computer. With HTML you can create and view Web pages on any computer platform (MAC or PC).

A set of special instructions, called HTML tags, are used to mark, or specify the format of, the text that is to be displayed on the Web page. Most, but not all, HTML tags come in pairs, with a *begin text* format and an *end text* format tag required. For instance, if you want to create a line of text that is bold face, you insert the text between the *begin bold* <B> and *end bold* </B> tags. Text that is to be italicized is inserted between the *begin italic* <I> and *end italic* </I> tags.

Numerous Web sites contain information on HTML programming. Some of those are listed below.

Setting up a Web Site for Your School: An Online Presentation
http://www.fred.net/nhhs/html2/present.htm

This guide is a starting point for school Web site generation and management. Visitors can download or distribute the documents found at this site as long as credit is given to the author and the Web site of North Hagerstown High School.

How Do They Do That with HTML?
http://www.nashville.net/~carl/htmlguide

Though content is truly the most important part of any Web page, aesthetics of the page are also important. Suggestions on this site may help with the aesthetics.

HTML Crash Course for Educators
http://edweb.cnidr.org/htmlintro.html

This tutorial will introduce you to the basics of HTML design and style. The *Crash Course* was originally designed with teachers in mind.

CERN—Web Authoring
http://www.cern.ch/WebOffice/Doc/OtherTools/AuthorTools.html

CERN contains Web authoring tutorials and links to many Web authoring sites. A non-exhaustive list of tools to use is categorized by platform. A series of HTML tutorials are available in collaboration with the IT/User Support group.

Classroom Internet Server Cookbook
http://web66.coled.umn.edu/Cookbook/Default.html

This is a cookbook that gives the recipes for setting up an Internet server in a classroom. Each recipe includes links so that you can download every ingredient that you need.

WHAT DOES A SAMPLE WEB PAGE LOOK LIKE IN HTML?

HTML code can be created by using a simple text editor, such as SimpleText on a MAC, or Notepad on Windows. Word processing software also can be used to write HTML code. There are three basic steps to creating a Web page:

1. Start your text editor and type in the HTML tags and text
2. Save the file with a .htm or .html extension
3. View the HTML file in a Web browser

There are a few HTML tags that make up a basic Web page, as listed below.

<HTML>
<HEAD>
<TITLE>
This is where a brief description of the purpose of the Web page is inserted. The text between the title tags displays on the title bar of the browser, rather than the Web page contents area.
</TITLE>
</HEAD>
<BODY>
This is where the content of the Web page is inserted. This text displays in the content area of the browser.
</BODY>
</HTML>

Other tags commonly used for Web page creation are:

HTML Tag	Purpose
<A></A>	Anchor tag; used to create hyperlinks
<CENTER></CENTER>	Centers text within the Web page window
<DD>	Definition part of a glossary list
<DL></DL>	A glossary definition list
<H1></H1>	Headings; range from H1 (largest) to H6 (smallest)
<HR>	Used to create a horizontal rule across the Web page
<LI>	Individual list items in ordered or unordered lists
<P></P>	A paragraph; inserts a blank line before the text
<OL></OL> or <UL></UL>	An order or unordered list; us <LI> tags for list items in both cases

If you see something on a Web page that you would like to incorporate into your own Web page, you can see how that page was created by viewing the source code of the page. You do this by selecting View from the menu bar and then select Source. Sites listed previously contain more HTML tags and their uses.

HOW CAN I CREATE MY OWN WEB PAGE?

Let's create a very simple Web page using HTML. The finished product is included for reference.

```
<HTML>
<HEAD>
<TITLE>
My Home Page
</TITLE>
</HEAD>
<BODY>
<CENTER><H1>Your Main Heading</H1></CENTER>
<P>Insert a paragraph of text here. Because of the paragraph tag used at the
beginning of this section, the text will display with a blank line preceding
it.</P>
<P>Another blank line is inserted between these sections. You can insert as
many paragraphs as you want.</P>
<UL>
<H2>A secondary, smaller heading</H2>
```

```
<LI>This is your first bullet item
<LI>This is your second bullet item
<LI>This is your last bullet item
</UL>
<DL>
<HR>
<H2>Creating hyperlinks</H2>
<P>The lines below contain the anchor tag with the hyperlink reference
(HREF) for the link and the text that is used to link.</P>
<DD>
<A HREF="http://www.whitehouse.gov">Visit the Whitehouse</A>
<DD>
<A HREF="http://www.ed.gov">U.S. Department of Education</A>
<DD>
<A HREF="http://www.matisse.net/files/glossary.html">Internet Terms</A>
</DL>
</BODY>
</HTML>
```

Once the HTML tags and your text are typed in, you need to save the file with a .htm or .html extension by clicking File on the menu bar of the text editor and then clicking Save. The filename must end with .htm or .html in order to be viewed in a browser. For this sample, name the file "homepage.htm."

Now that the file is saved, it can be viewed in your browser by clicking File on the menu bar of the browser and then clicking Open. Type the filename that you gave when you saved the file (homepage.htm) into the address text box of the browser and press the Enter key. With the few lines of HTML code above, you created the Web page shown on the next page.

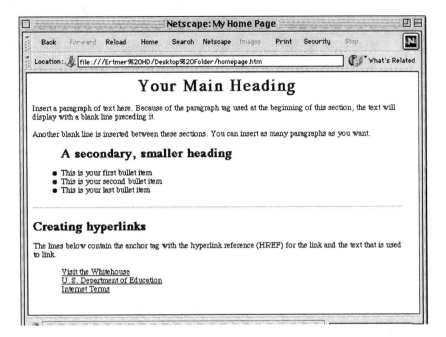

Your Main Heading

Insert a paragraph of text here. Because of the paragraph tag used at the beginning of this section, the text will display with a blank line preceding it.

Another blank line is inserted between these sections. You can insert as many paragraphs as you want.

A secondary, smaller heading

- This is your first bullet item
- This is your second bullet item
- This is your last bullet item

Creating hyperlinks

The lines below contain the anchor tag with the hyperlink reference (HREF) for the link and the text that is used to link.

Visit the Whitehouse
U. S. Department of Education
Internet Terms

Sample page

SUMMARY

The World Wide Web is as extensive as it is today because of the Web pages that have been published over the last 10 years. Educators are getting more involved with the Web today by creating Web pages for themselves, their classes, or together with their students. Many of the most popular and interesting Web sites are those that have been created by individual classes or teachers. Contributing information to the Web is becoming an important role for everyone in the field of education.

SECTION 3:
ACCESS TO CURRICULAR CONNECTIONS

The Internet offers an incredible array of resources for teachers who wish to transform their curricula by incorporating the sights, sounds, and experiences offered through the Web. For example, the Internet allows students to:

- interact with people from other countries and cultures
- compile an investment portfolio
- take a tour of the circulatory system
- dissect a frog
- interact with NASA scientists
- access real data (e.g., census, weather, investment)
- participate, virtually, in critical historical events
- develop research and writing skills
- publish literary and art work

Of course, these examples barely scratch the surface of the possibilities available. Students can visit other countries, converse with famous authors and scientists, take virtual tours of famous art and historical museums, interact with other students, and even get help with their homework. The problem is that there are so many sites available that it's hard to know where to begin.

When teachers first start using the Internet as a curriculum resource, they tend to work within established content areas. For that reason, this chapter is organized around common school subjects. Within each content area, we point you to some of the best Web sites available. In addition, most of these sites lead to other sites with related information.

HOW CAN THE WORLD WIDE WEB ENGAGE STUDENTS IN MATH?

The Web offers multiple opportunities for students to explore the mathematical concepts involved in everyday situations. The sites listed here range from those geared toward primary students to those intended for secondary and post-secondary students.

Mega Mathematics
http://www.cs.uidaho.edu/~casey931/mega-math/

MegaMath makes challenging and interesting topics in math and computer science (algorithms, infinity, logic) accessible to elementary school kids. This site includes lots of stories, games, and projects on a variety of topics. By incorporating interactivity and exploiting the available technology, *MegaMath* creates interesting and fun math-based Web materials.

Ask Dr. Math
http://forum.swarthmore.edu/dr.math/index.html

Have a math question? If so, then check out *Ask Dr. Math.* Dr. Math is a question and answer service for K–12 students and their teachers. Users can explore a searchable archive by level and topic, as well as a section devoted to Frequently Asked Questions (FAQs).

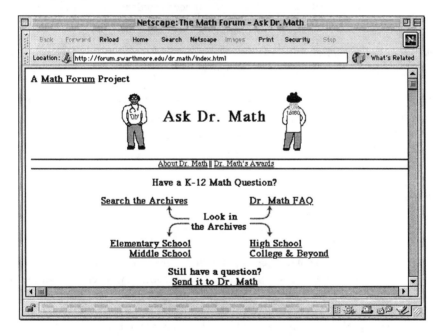

MathMagic

http://forum.swarthmore.edu/mathmagic/

MathMagic is a K–12 telecommunications project developed in El Paso, Texas, and hosted by the Math Forum. It combines students' use of computer technology with the development of problem-solving strategies and communications skills. *MathMagic* posts challenges in each of four grade categories (K–3, 4–6, 7–9, and 10–12) and encourages each registered team to pair up with another team and engage in a problem-solving dialogue. When an agreement is reached, one solution is posted for every pair.

PlaneMath

http://www.planemath.com

PlaneMath makes math educational materials readily accessible to students with disabilities, particularly physical disabilities. This site is designed specifically to stimulate and motivate special needs students in grades 4–7 to pursue aeronautics-related careers.

What Good Is Math?

http://www.richmond.edu/~ed344/96/math/

This site, created by pre-service math teachers at the University of Richmond, provides middle school students with everyday examples of math-in-use. Examples relate to common teenager experiences including art, finance, grades, and cooking.

Investing for Kids

http://tqd.advanced.org/3096/index.htm

This site, designed by middle and high school students, includes activities for learners at all levels (elementary through college). *Investing for Kids* teaches the principles of saving and investing to both beginners and seasoned investors by examining stocks, bonds, and mutual funds. An exciting feature of this site is the inclusion of a stock market game that helps users learn how to invest. In addition to reading about the concepts of investing, students can use the Java goal calculator, take a financial quiz, put together a stock portfolio, check out the stock learning center, look up terms in the glossary, and find out about collaborative projects.

U.S. Treasury Page for Kids

http://www.ustreas.gov/kids/
http://www.ustreas.gov/kids/kidsmoney.html

This page is geared, primarily, toward elementary and middle school students. Besides taking a tour of the U.S. Treasury Building and learning about its history, students can engage in a variety of interactive activities including determining the current worth of a variety of savings bonds, starting a business, earning wages, paying taxes, and investing money.

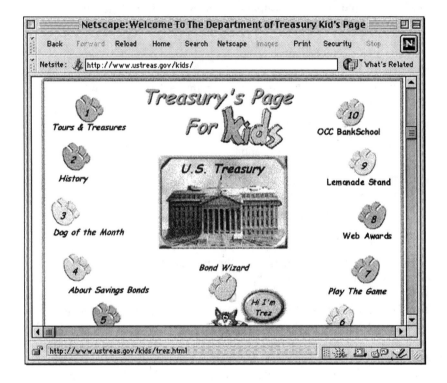

21ˢᵗ Century Problem Solving
http://www2.hawaii.edu/suremath/home.html

This site is dedicated to promoting problem solving skills across the curriculum, with a particular emphasis on pre-college algebra. These Web pages provide examples of problems that have been solved using reliable problem solving methods; discussion of the principles of reliable problem solving; and an evolving encyclopedia of solved problems in mathematics, physics, and chemistry.

On-line Mathematics from Lopaka's Notebook—Robert Garry
http://gauss.hawcc.hawaii.edu/maths/maths.html

This site embeds mathematical principles and concepts within everyday phenomena and real-world problems. Geared primarily toward pre-calculus students, this site provides resources that might not be available otherwise. Some of the projects include:

- How Long Will the Oil Last? (Functions)
- The Stardust Mission (Equations)
- The Parabola (Polynomials)
- Tidal Energy (Applications of Trig Functions)
- The Great Balsa Bridge Contest (Vector Analysis)
- The Chaos Game (Sequences and Limits)
- Bicycle Helmet Safety (Probability and Statistics)

National Council of Teachers of Mathematics (NCTM)
http://www.nctm.org/about/

The National Council of Teachers of Mathematics is the largest nonprofit professional association of mathematics educators, dedicated to improving the teaching and learning of mathematics. NCTM offers vision, leadership, and communication avenues for mathematics educators at the elementary, middle, and high school levels, as well as college and university levels. At the NCTM site, you will find information about the latest edition of the mathematics standards, related conferences, as well as links to other sites that include lesson plans, activities, and projects.

The Internet provides tremendous opportunities for updating and enriching the traditional textbook-based curriculum. In the area of science, massive amounts of real-time information are available. For example, pictures from Mars, interviews with noted scientists, live experiments, and monitoring of weather changes are all readily available through the World Wide Web.

Exemplary Projects Integrating Math and Science for Elementary, Middle, and High School Students
http://www.ncrel.org/mands/lessons.htm

This site is a great example of one that provides multiple links to other related sites. This site was created by the Midwest Consortium for Mathematics and Science Education to link educators to activities that reflect a commitment to constructivist-based learning. As the result, students have the opportunity to engage in a variety of meaningful and purposeful activities in both math and science.

The Heart: An Online Exploration
http://sln2.fi.edu/biosci/heart.html

Designed for multiple grade levels, this Web site allows learners to explore the wonders of the human heart. Students can follow the blood through the vessels or wander through the web-like body systems. They also can learn about how to have a healthy heart and how to monitor their heart's health. If they have the stomach for it, students can even watch a video of heart bypass surgery.

Neuroscience for Kids
http://weber.u.washington.edu/~chudler/neurok.html

This site helps students and teachers learn more about the nervous system by participating in activities and experiments related to memory and learning, sleep and dream patterns, sidedness, reflexes, and more. If you have a question about the nervous system, the "Neuroscientist Network" offers one way to find the answer. A unique feature of this site is that you can keep track of information you find by using an embedded notebook feature. After your notes are compiled you simply email the information to yourself.

VolcanoWorld

http://volcano.und.edu

VolcanoWorld is designed for anyone who has a special interest in volcanoes. The University of North Dakota first posted the site in 1995 and since then it has averaged 8,000 visitors per day. While visiting the site you can ask a volcanologist a question, view the most recent eruptions around the world, find out about volcano-related conferences, locate lesson plans, and even participate in volcano-related games.

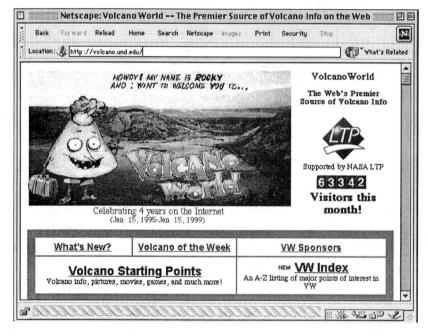

National Wildlife Federation (NWF)
http://www.nwf.org/nwf/index.html

NWF focuses its efforts on five core issues (Endangered Habitat, Water Quality, Land Stewardship, Wetlands, and Sustainable Communities), and pursues a range of educational projects within each of these core areas.

NWF's Animal Tracks® program (http://www.nwf.org/nwf/atracks/) offers both online and printed conservation education materials to elementary and middle school teachers and students who are learning about the environment and how to care for it.

NWF's National Wildlife Week program (http://www.nwf.org/nwf/wildlifeweek/) offers free conservation curriculum materials to teachers and their students. This site also has a page (http://www.nwf.org/kids/) devoted to kids' activities and includes links to games, Ranger Rick, tours of the wetlands, and quizzes to see how much was learned.

The Natural History Museum of London
http://www.nhm.ac.uk/interactive.html

This site, designed for middle and high school students, includes a variety of interactive science activities. Students are invited to participate in QUEST (Questioning, Understanding and Exploring Simulated Things) and explore twelve of the Museum's fascinating objects using "virtual" tools. In the Science Casebook, students discover the Beast of Bodmin Moor, learn how to identify meteorites, and consider the question of whether we can recreate dinosaurs. Through the Museum's extensive Dinosaur Data Files, students can access virtual card files on all the popular dinosaurs.

Carnegie Science Academy
http://csa.clpgh.org/

The *Carnegie Science Academy* Web site is an interactive environment where high school students can explore science and technology in an online social environment. As a professional society for teens with a special interest in science, The *Carnegie Science Academy* encourages independent thinking, science exploration, professional development, and interpersonal skills. This site provides students with the foundations to explore and enhance an interest in science while also providing services that schools typically do not have the time to give.

NASA's Educational Program
http://www.nasa.gov
http://www.hq.nasa.gov/office/codef/education/index.html

NASA's space missions produce new data, images, and information that may be effectively included in teachers' curricula. NASA collaborates with professional education associations, state and local education authorities, universities, private enterprise, and other organizations to develop instructional products that are consistent with the national curriculum standards and/or state or local curriculum frameworks. NASA's products are developed in multiple formats, with an emphasis on innovative applications of educational technology and interactive strategies.

The National Space Science Data Center
http://nssdc.gsfc.nasa.gov/

The National Space Science Data Center (NSSDC) provides access to a wide variety of astrophysics, space physics, solar physics, lunar and planetary data from NASA space flight missions. Spacecraft and experiments that have or will provide public access data are also accessible through NSSCD. There are multiple links to photographic images, publications, and other outer space sites.

Solar System Simulator
http://space.jpl.nasa.gov/

The *Solar System Simulator* is a collaborative project of NASA, the Jet Propulsion Laboratory (JPL), and the California State Polytechnic University that offers a "spyglass on the cosmos." The Web-based simulator can create a color image of any planet or satellite as seen from any point in the solar system. The Simulator is currently being used by the Shuttle Radar Topography, Cassini, Galileo, and other missions for trajectory animation and mission visualization.

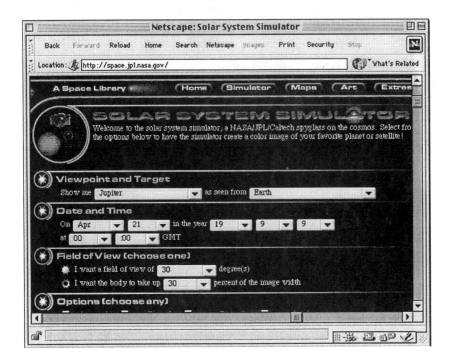

National Science Teachers Association (NSTA)
http://www.nsta.org

NSTA is the largest organization in the world committed to promoting
excellence and innovation in science teaching and learning. To address
subjects of critical interest to science educators, the Association publishes
five journals, a newspaper, many books, a children's magazine called
Dragonfly, and many other publications. NSTA conducts national and
regional conventions that attract more than 30,000 attendees annually
including science teachers and supervisors, administrators, scientists, and
business and industry representatives involved in science education.

Technology offers teachers and students the opportunity to interact with social sciences content (history, social studies, geography, civics, and economics) in ways that build increased understandings of world politics and geography. The Internet allows students to interact with voluminous amounts of timely information as well as with students from classrooms around the world.

Kids Web Japan
http://jin.jcic.or.jp/kidsweb/

Kids Web Japan introduces students, ages 10–14, to the sights and sounds of Japan. This site provides a wonderful source of information for teachers and students who are studying the culture of Japan. Numerous photographs and graphics are also included.

National Geographic World
http://www.nationalgeographic.com/world/index.html

Here's a site where children can engage in a variety of fun activities, either as part of a social studies unit or as an after-school or free-time activity. At this site they can:

- discuss their favorite books in the BookWorm Corner
- read stories from the World magazine and submit their own story ideas for a future issue
- join the pen pal network (GeoMail)
- explore the virtual solar system
- add their own cartoons to the cartoon factory collection

If you're looking for something a little more advanced, National Geographic's home page (www.nationalgeographic.com) links to pages of their premier magazine. You can also explore the National Geographic Society (NGS) in other interesting ways:

- search an index of publications or visit the library
- meet recipients of NGS's research grants
- pay a virtual visit to the museum or take in a lecture
- learn what it takes to win the National Geography Bee

- pose a question to the staff or check the mini-encyclopedia
- explore NGS's newest book, kids magazine, or travel magazine

Where on the Globe Is Roger?
http://www.gsn.org/roger/index.html

Elementary and middle school children learn about history, culture, and geography while they travel electronically with Roger Williams, a retired Airline Pilot and U.S. Marine Corps Aviator, as he drives his truck from continent to continent around the world. During his travels, Roger visits schools, meeting students and teachers and sending greetings and reports on his travels back to the classes participating in the "Where on the Globe Is Roger?" project.

WebQuests
http://edweb.sdsu.edu/EdWeb_Folder/courses/EDTEC596/About_WebQuests.html

WebQuests have become a popular educational activity, especially within the social studies area. According to Bernie Dodge (see URL above) a WebQuest is "an inquiry-oriented activity in which some or all of the information that learners interact with comes from resources on the Internet." The primary purpose of a WebQuest is to challenge students with an authentic task, provide them with multiple resources, support higher-level thinking through active learning, and have them work collaboratively to complete a task. Critical attributes of a WebQuest include:

- an introduction
- a task
- a set of information sources needed to complete the task
- a description of the process learners should go through in completing the task
- guidance on how to organize the information
- a conclusion that brings closure to the quest

An excellent example is provided by the following Web site.

Searching for China: WebQuest
http://www.kn.pacbell.com/wired/China/ChinaQuest.html

Searching for China is a rich, meaning-centered experience that, through the power of the Internet, actively engages students in the culture of China. Specifically, students who complete this particular WebQuest are expected to:

- develop an interest in the study of China
- use the Internet for advanced exploration of China
- learn about six key aspects of Chinese culture
- view complex topics from various perspectives
- formulate and support an argument from one of six perspectives
- work with teammates to solve a combined action plan
- question the nature of international relations in our interdependent world

Social Science Data Collection
http://ssdc.ucsd.edu/index.html

SSDC is a collection of numeric data in the social sciences maintained by the Social Sciences and Humanities Library of University of California, San Diego. Students can engage in online data analysis and use spreadsheet applications to examine U.S. budget information, population and housing data, and current demographic data.

SCORE: Schools of California Online Resources
http://score.rims.k12.ca.us/

Funded by the California Technology Assistance Project, these history-social science resources have been selected and evaluated by a team of California educators. These sites were chosen for their accuracy, grade appropriateness, and richness of content. This site also includes links to grade-leveled lessons; curricula frameworks, content-based standards, and assessment measures; professional development resources; and virtual projects and field trips.

The Internet Newspaper
http://www.trib.com/NEWS/

This site links to all of your favorite sources of world and national news including ABC News, *The New York Times*, and CNN.

How Far Is It?
http://www.indo.com/distance/

This service uses data from the U.S. Census Bureau and a supplementary list of cities from around the world to find the latitude and longitude of two places, and then calculates the distance between them (as the crow flies). It also provides a map showing the two places using the Xerox PARC Map.

Walk a Mile in My Shoes: Multicultural Curriculum Resources
http://ernie.wmht.org/trail/explor02.htm

Walk a Mile in My Shoes is a year-long language curriculum that uses literature to teach children to know, understand, and respect others by recognizing similarities among people while appreciating differences. Links are provided to a variety of resources that can be used to enhance a multicultural curriculum including sites for kids and teachers, sites on

61

multiculturalism, sites on children's literature, and sites for students to meet other students.

Smithsonian Institution National Museum of the American Indian
http://www.si.edu/nmai/

This site provides the opportunity for teachers and students to take a virtual field trip to the *Smithsonian's National Museum of the American Indian.* This museum is dedicated to the preservation, study, and exhibition of the life, languages, literature, history, and arts of Native Americans. The museum's collections span more than 10,000 years of Native American heritage, from ancient stone Clovis points to modern silkscreen prints.

The American Immigration Home Page
http://www.bergen.org/AAST/Projects/Immigration/index.html

The *American Immigration Home Page* was started as a part of a school project for a 10th grade American History class. The project provides information about how immigrants were treated, and also why they decided to come to America.

National Museum of Women's History
http://www.nmwh.org/home_frames.html

The National Museum of Women's History in Washington, DC, is a nonpartisan, nonprofit educational institution dedicated to preserving and celebrating the historic contributions and the rich, diverse heritage of women. NMWH focuses on the history of women in the Americas in the context of world history. As part of its efforts, a monument honoring women's suffrage has been raised in the U.S. Capitol.

Directory of Social Studies, Social Science, Art, & Music Education-Related Organizations
http://www.indiana.edu/~ssdc/orgs.htm

This directory lists non-commercial organizations, including professional organizations, concerned with the social studies, social sciences, art education, music education, or related topics. Many of these organizations publish curriculum and teaching guides, lesson plans, journals, and magazines; conduct conventions, conferences, teacher workshops and seminars; and offer other types of services, support, and resources for educators. This site includes links to the U.S. Department of Education, the National Council for the Social Studies, The National Library of Education, and the Ackerman Center for Democratic Education, located at Purdue University.

HOW CAN THE WORLD WIDE WEB ENGAGE STUDENTS IN
LITERACY AND LANGUAGE ARTS?

The World Wide Web provides powerful support for both reading and writing activities. Students seem particularly motivated to write well when they have an audience who will read their work. In addition, students can interact with both famous and obscure authors, access writing resources, and even play language games that sharpen important skills.

Kids' Web—A WWW Digital Library for Schoolkids
http://www.npac.syr.edu/textbook/kidsweb/

The goal of *Kid's Web* is to provide students with access to a subset of the Web that is simple to navigate. Each subject section contains a list of links to information that is understandable and interesting to school kids. There are also links to external lists of material on each subject which more advanced students can browse for further information. If you take the Arts link to the Literature link you will find sections on children's books, including online books, children's authors, fictional works, creative writing resources, as well as resources that allow you to explore the worlds of poetry and theater.

The Children's Literature Web Guide
http://www.acs.ucalgary.ca/~dkbrown/index.html

The *Children's Literature Web Guide* gathers and categorizes the growing number of Internet resources related to books for children and young adults. Much of the information on these pages is provided by fans, schools, libraries, and commercial businesses involved in the book world. Links to current book awards are also included.

Lit Cafe
http://hyperion.advanced.org/17500/

The *Lit Cafe* uses the metaphor of a coffee house to guide students, teachers, and other interested persons through the basics of literature, all within an intriguing and informative setting. This virtual classroom allows visitors to read biographies of famous authors or their works; play CafeLibs, a version of MadLibs; and submit their own work to the bulletin board.

WhyPoetryWhat: An Internet Sampler on Poetry
http://www.kn.pacbell.com/wired/fil/pages/samwhypoetrmi.html

This Web site introduces students to various aspects of poetry. The site uses several resources available on the Web to help students become more familiar with poetry as an art form. There are links to Web sites on rhyming, limerick rules, and more. Activities can be completed alone or in small groups.

Author's Pen
http://www.books.com/scripts/authors.exe

This site currently includes more than 1,000 authors, and it's still growing. Each listing includes a brief biography, a bibliography, and, when available, links to audio interviews and readings, as well as Web site and email addresses.

Laura Ingalls Wilder, Frontier Girl
http://webpages.marshall.edu/~irby1/laura.htmlx

This Web site is devoted to the life and works of Laura Ingalls Wilder, American pioneer and children's author of the famous "Little House" books. Designed to provide information about Ms. Wilder and the places and characters mentioned in her books, this site is interactive, informational, and entertaining.

Into the Wardrobe: The C. S. Lewis WWW site (1898-1998)
http://cslewis.DrZeus.net/

Developed by a fan of C. S. Lewis, this Web site began as a short list of books written by Lewis and grew as a result of the contributions of others. The site includes links to a biography of Lewis, sound and photo links, message forums, chat rooms, other related Web sites, and personal anecdotes contributed by friends and relatives of C. S. Lewis.

The Grammar Gorillas
http://www.funbrain.com/grammar/

Grammar Gorillas, geared toward helping students identify parts of speech, is just one activity students will like at the FunBrain site (http://www.funbrain.com/index.html). Other language arts activities include: creating word search puzzles, playing hangman, finding misspelled words, learning new words, and writing stories.

Kid Crosswords and Other Puzzles
http://www.kidcrosswords.com/

Kid Crosswords and Other Puzzles provides educators and parents with free puzzles that are designed to develop children's minds. Although "fun" puzzles are published, the primary goal is to provide creative and high-quality educational resources. Posted puzzles focus on a specific topic (civil rights, Africa, division). The most popular subjects are holidays, English, math, history, and geography, in that order. All kinds of puzzles are available: word search, rebus, crossword, scramble, connect-the-dots, and picture builders, to name a few.

Copyright (1999) by Brian Goss. Reprinted with permission.

Online Writing Lab (OWL)
http://owl.english.purdue.edu/

If you need help with your writing, Purdue University's *Online Writing Lab* is available 24 hours a day. OWL offers resources on writing skills, resources for students learning English as a second language, and resources on writing resumes. Over 125 handouts on writing skills are available to help students hone their skills. Teachers can also find links to writing-related resources, style guides, children's resources, and professional writing organizations.

National Council of Teachers of English
http://www.ncte.org

The National Council of Teachers of English is devoted to improving the teaching and learning of English and the language arts at all levels of education. Individual members are teachers and supervisors of English programs in elementary and secondary schools, faculty in college and university English departments, teacher educators, local and state agency English specialists, and professionals in related fields. This page leads to many other related sites including the national standards for English and a large collection of teaching ideas and materials.

HOW CAN THE WORLD WIDE WEB ENGAGE STUDENTS IN ART, MUSIC, AND PHYSICAL EDUCATION?

Technology has always played a part in the arts by providing the tools, materials, and processes to facilitate artists' creative expression. Also, Web sites related to physical education provide invaluable resources from which students, coaches, teachers, and parents will benefit.

Kids' Corner: Kids' Art
http://kids.ot.com/

This site is devoted to publishing kids' stories, poems, artwork, crafts, and photography. The site is intended primarily for students ages 1–16. New exhibits are published weekly. The kid art gallery has a particularly nice collection of work.

Make a Splash with Color
http://www.thetech.org/exhibits_events/online/color/intro/

This Web site has three main sections: Talking about Color, The Lighter Side of Color, and An Eye on Color. Through a variety of activities and exhibits, students can explore different "ingredients of color," can observe the way color changes when it is reflected off objects or routed through tinted lenses, and can understand why our eyes sometimes see the "wrong" color!

ArtsEdNet

http://www.artsednet.getty.edu/

ArtsEdNet is an online service developed by the Getty Education Institute for the Arts, to support the needs of the K–12 arts education community. It focuses on helping arts educators, general classroom teachers using the arts in their curriculum, museum educators, and university faculty involved in the arts. *ArtsEdNet* disseminates information through the Internet and encourages the exchange of ideas and experiences regarding advocacy and professional, curriculum, and theory development.

Artswire Web Base

http://www.artswire.org/webbase/main.cgi

Artswire is a self-service database of cultural resources, created as a public service for the online arts community to keep abreast of new arts sites and for arts Websters to promote their new or renovated sites to a targeted audience vitally interested in the arts. Users can access an automatic registry form to announce their own arts and cultural sites.

Arts: Blacksbury Electronic Village

http://www.bev.net/community/arts.html

This site includes multiple relevant links to online art exhibits, education in the arts, art organizations, as well as museums, theaters, galleries and even night clubs.

Worldwide Internet Music Resources

http://www.music.indiana.edu/music_resources/

This site is maintained by the William and Gayle Cook Music Library of the Indiana University School of Music. Visitors can link to any of the following topics:

- Individual Musicians (all genres) and Popular Groups
- Groups and Ensembles (except Popular)
- Other Sites Related to Performance
- Composers and Composition
- Genres and Types of Music
- Research and Study
- The Commercial World of Music

- Journals and Magazines
- General and Miscellaneous

MusicNet
http://tqd.advanced.org/3306/

Within three main sections (MusicNet Encyclopedia, MusicNet Professions, and MusicNet Interactive) of the *MusicNet* Web site, visitors can learn about music education in a fun and educational manner. *MusicNet* features online games, message forums and real-time chat, a music encyclopedia with over 100 terms, and interesting music education facts.

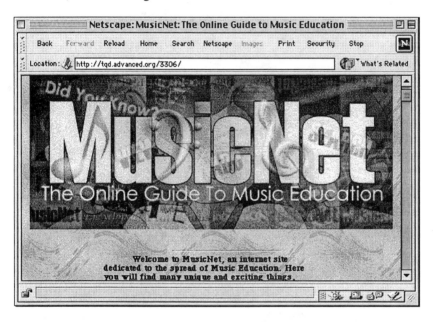

Music Notes: An Interactive Online Musical Experience
http://library.advanced.org/15413/

This site is designed to enhance music education for students of all ages. Topics include music theory, music history, and careers in music. Visitors can explore a variety of musical professions, learn how to read music, read about different instruments, and explore musical styles from Bach to Rock. A glossary and message board are also included.

Classical Midi Archives
http://www.prs.net/midi.html

This site contains over 7000 classical MIDI files from over 500 composers. MIDI refers to the Musical Instrument Digital Interface—a standard format that enables computers, electronic musical instruments, and software to communicate with each other. At this site the files are organized into three main categories:

- main composers (219)
- other composers (221)
- other (encores, timelines, inspirations and aspirations).

Users can also access free software including MidiGate (a mid player with unlimited queing), the world clock, and even a screen saver which is also a game.

Piano on the Net '97
http://www.artdsm.com/music.html

Students can learn how to play the piano by completing a series of lessons on the net. Each lesson takes about 35 minutes to complete. Students are encouraged to work slowly and at their own pace. Each lesson should be mastered before beginning the next.

PE Central
http://pe.central.vt.edu/

PE Central is designed for physical education teachers, students, interested parents and adults. The goal is to provide the latest information about contemporary, developmentally appropriate physical education programs for children and youth. Visitors are encouraged to submit their own lesson ideas that will be reviewed by the editorial board. The site includes links to assessment ideas, adapted PE lesson plans and equipment sources, cool Web sites, health and nutrition ideas, and outdoor recreation activities.

President's Challenge—Youth Physical Fitness Program
http://www.indiana.edu/~preschal/

This Web site provides information about the President's Challenge Fitness and Health award programs including criteria and guidelines for special needs students, homeschools, and demonstration centers. Events and standards for each level of award are provided. Links to fitness-related sites (report from the Surgeon General, Physical Activity and Fitness Research Digest) are also included.

Fitness Files
http://chitrib.webpoint.com/fitness/

This Web site has four main areas to navigate: Fitness Fundamentals, Get Active, The Injurenet, and Fuel for Fitness. Within these links, students learn the basic principles of fitness, how to calculate their target heart rates, which activities can help them stay active, how to stretch properly, and what foods are essential for a healthy diet.

SUMMARY

The Internet and the World Wide Web are ideal resources for teachers and students who are interested in interacting with people, resources, and curricula at deeper levels than previously possible. Even though the resources listed in this section don't begin to represent all that is available, they provide a wonderful place to start. No matter what subject or what grade level you teach, you will find some of the best resources represented here. And if you're wondering how to begin, it's really quite simple. Just point your mouse and click!

SECTION 4: MAKING ACCESS EQUITABLE, SAFE, AND RESPONSIBLE

As teachers start *planning* to use the Internet within their classrooms a number of issues arise that must be addressed immediately, even *before* access is obtained. These issues revolve around three main concerns: access, safety, and responsibility. Teachers must assume primary responsibility for educating themselves and their students about all three areas of concern.

First, educators must help ensure that students have "equitable access;" that is, resources must be technologically and financially available to all students regardless of location, distance, resources, or disability. Failure to provide equal access can lead to a growing gap between the information "haves" and "have nots." Teachers must continue to make efforts to prevent this type of situation, which currently exists in many locations, from escalating.

The second issue relates to safety. Use of the Internet must not compromise students' safety. Although schools must help prevent students from being unnecessarily exposed to objectionable material on the Internet, students must also act to ensure their own safety by following both their school's guidelines, as well as the informal guidelines that govern online behavior (i.e., the rules of Netiquette). Achieving safe use requires that all users act appropriately, although, in reality, this is not likely to happen. According to Schrum and Berenfeld (1997) efforts are currently being made "to resolve these issues both politically and legally without challenging First Amendment rights" (p. 114).

The third issue relates to responsibility. When teachers and students use the Internet responsibly, they take care to evaluate the information that they access, to check for accuracy and value, and to give credit to those whose work they use. "Although there are laws and conventions to address traditional copyright infringements, plagiarism, privacy issues, document tampering, and individuals freedom, similar conventions are rare in the world of digital information" (Schrum & Berenfeld, p. 117).

By discussing all of these issues with students *before* they access the Internet, many problems (although certainly not all) can be avoided. This section is designed to increase your awareness of the importance of each issue, as well as to identify ways to eliminate or manage the potential problems.

73

One of the best things about the Internet is that it allows you to connect with people and resources around the world. One minute you can be sitting in your classroom in Coeur d'Alene, Idaho (http://www.sd271.k12.id.us/winton/), and the next minute you are on a virtual field trip to the Smithsonian Astrophysical Observatory in Cambridge, Massachusetts (http://cfa-www.harvard.edu/sao-home.html). Just a moment later, you are touring the National Museum of Science and Technology in Ottawa, Canada (http://www.digimark.net/iatech). It's almost as easy as snapping your fingers. Or is it?

Have you ever tried to connect with students in rural Arkansas? Although they might have computers, do they have access to the Internet? What if you want to connect with students in South Western Africa? They may not have access to telephone lines, let alone computers. How about connecting with students at the Colorado School for the Deaf and Blind? Can they truly receive the information that you have posted on your colorful, interactive Web pages? As these examples have pointed out, not everyone enjoys equal access to these wonderful electronic resources. Not only is connectivity a problem in some areas of the world, but for special populations, access to these resources can be difficult if not impossible to achieve due to poor screen design, "untagged" images, poor navigational aids, and so on. As future Web developers, these are important issues for you to consider.

HOW CAN I MAKE WEB RESOURCES ACCESSIBLE TO SPECIAL POPULATIONS?

People with disabilities deserve the same easy access to electronic information and resources as everyone else. For example, people with poor vision can benefit from Web resources if Web developers think to incorporate textual representations of their images and video files within their pages. Similarly, people with hearing impairments can benefit from textual representations of audio files. It takes but a little forethought during the development process to achieve a higher level of accessibility. Web developers (including you and your students) can find suggestions on the Internet for how to make Web pages more readily accessible to people with special needs. Some helpful Web sites are included on the following pages.

EASI: Equal Access to Software and Information
http://www.rit.edu/~easi

EASI serves as a resource to the education community by providing
information and guidance in the area of access-to-information technologies
by individuals with disabilities. EASI stays informed about developments and
advancements within the adaptive computer technology field and spreads that
information to colleges, universities, K–12 schools, libraries, and into the
workplace. EASI promotes equal access through on-site and online
workshops, publications, videos, email discussion lists, an information-rich
Web site, electronic journal, and through participation in a wide variety of
regional and national conferences.

Center for Applied Special Technologies
http://www.cast.org/

The Center for Applied Special Technologies (CAST) provides suggestions
for how to make Web-based resources available to people worldwide.
According to CAST, these suggestions "are not 'workarounds,' nor do they
require a sacrifice of design elements to achieve. Some are enhancements to
traditional Web sites, such as image and sound descriptions. Others are
simply appropriate uses of common Web design elements such as graphical
navigation, tables, and the wording of text." Through the use of universal
design elements, CAST strives to provide Web sites that are useful, well
designed, and universally accessible. The design principles that CAST
suggests include:

1. ALT-tags and picture descriptions for all images
2. Text equivalent of all sound and video files
3. Graphical and textual representations of navigation system on all
   pages
4. Color coding of pages by the sections in which they are found for
   easy identification
5. External links open in new window
6. Index and "back to index" links
7. Text versions of tables
8. Text access
9. Inclusion of new html 4.0 accessibility tags (for Web Accessibility
   Initiative [WAI] page author guidelines working group, see
   http://www.w3.org/wai/gl/)
10. Cascading style sheets

Bobby

http://www.cast.org/bobby/

To determine if a Web site is universally accessible, use "Bobby," a Web-based public service offered by CAST that analyzes Web pages for their accessibility to people with disabilities as well as their compatibility with various browsers. To display the "Bobby Approved" icon, all pages on the Web site must meet the requirements outlined in the guidelines on page 75.

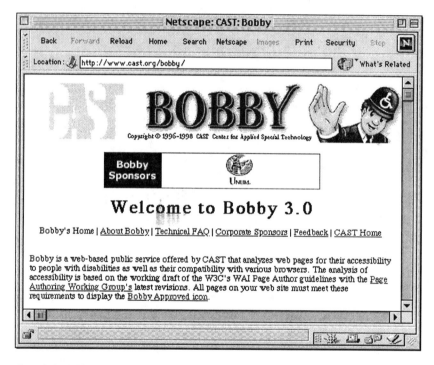

Copyright (1996-1999) by CAST. Reprinted with permission.

WebABLE!
http://www.yuri.org/webable/index.html

WebABLE! Solutions provides links to Web accessibility tools including voice browsers and screen readers, as well as links to legal standards supporting accessibility. *WebABLE!* states that its mission is to "stimulate education, research and development of technologies that will ensure accessibility for people with disabilities to advanced information systems and emerging technologies." This site also includes a database that lists hundreds of Internet-based resources related to accessibility.

HOW CAN I DEVELOP WEB-BASED LESSONS THAT ARE UNIVERSALLY ACCESSIBLE?

Model for Development of Accessible Web-Based Science Lessons
http://www.cast.org/initiatives/modelwebsciencelessons.html

The Center for Applied Special Technologies (CAST) has teamed up with Agassiz Elementary School in Boston to create "The Model for Developing Accessible Web-Based Science Lessons." This model supports teachers' development and use of accessible Web-based Science lessons in two ways. First teachers learn how to locate and select educationally sound science information on the Web that is consistent with their approved curriculum standards. Second, they learn how to use special software to make the selected sites accessible to students with disabilities and low reading skills. By becoming familiar with the implications of accessibility standards, teachers learn both how and why to create their own accessible materials.

Impact! Online
http://lrs.ed.uiuc.edu/Impact/

Impact! Online is an interactive news magazine for intermediate and advanced ESL/EFL (English-as-a-Second Language/English-as a-Foreign-Language) students. This Web site features articles about current events, health, sports, and entertainment. In each article, certain words are highlighted. If you click on any of these words, you will be linked to an explanation page for that word. Some of these pages feature audio files, which help students pronounce the word. They also have a mailing list which students can join if they would like to discuss *Impact! Online* with other readers.

Accessibility issues extend beyond the needs of special populations. Accessibility also relates to connecting with people in rural areas of the United States, as well as people in other countries.

Intercultural E-Mail Classroom Connections (IECC)
http://www.iecc.org

IECC is a free service that helps teachers link with partners in other countries and cultures for e-mail classroom pen-pal and project exchanges. Since its creation in 1992, IECC has distributed over 21,000 requests for e-mail partnerships. At last count, more than 7,100 teachers in 79 countries were participating in one or more of the IECC lists.

Web66: International School Web Site Registry
http://web66.coled.umn.edu/schools.html

Web66 maintains the Internet's oldest and most complete list of school Web servers, including schools in Australia, Africa, Canada, Europe, and Japan. Visitors can search by level of school as well as by special categories such as Parochial, Handicapped, Montessori, Gifted and Talented, and Online.

SUMMARY

As you start creating your own Web pages, it is important to keep in mind the issue of equal access. It doesn't take a lot of extra effort to assure that the Web sites you develop are accessible to users who have physical or sensory limitations. Ensuring access for people in rural areas or developing countries will be more difficult to resolve. However, through an increased awareness of these issues, we can begin to consider ways to minimize access difficulties so that everyone has an equal opportunity to enjoy these rich resources.

As with print media, it is important to protect students from objectionable information. Because of the amount of information on the Internet, and the ease with which students can access it, assuring safety is a difficult task.

There are both formal and informal guidelines that are designed to keep students safe when using the Internet. Informal guidelines refer to the rules of proper behavior on the Internet. These are commonly known as Netiquette (Network Etiquette) and include rules such as:

- avoid abusive or foul language
- do not interfere with another person's e-mail
- refrain from sending inappropriate messages
- avoid typing in all caps . . . IT SEEMS LIKE YOU'RE SHOUTING!

Formal guidelines, referred to as Acceptable Use Policies (AUPs), are discussed below.

WHAT IS ACCEPTABLE USE ON THE INTERNET?

With Internet access becoming more and more common within our schools, a clear set of guidelines must be in place. These guidelines, or AUPs, are used to guide proper use of the Internet by students, teachers, administrators, parents, and board members. An AUP needs to specifically state what type of Internet use is acceptable, and what steps will be taken if the Internet is used in an unacceptable manner. Day and Schrum (1995) define an AUP as "a written agreement signed by students, their parents, and their teachers outlining the terms and conditions of Internet use . . .." The AUP encompasses "rules of online behaviors and access privileges" (p. 9).

There are two primary reasons for creating a school AUP:

- to protect children and adolescents from inappropriate material
- to protect the school system from litigation

Day and Schrum devised a checklist of issues that an AUP must address (1995, p. 9). These guidelines include:

- define the Internet in simple terms
- outline the Netiquette rules that students must follow
- address ethical and legal issues, including copyright laws
- define objectionable material in the same manner used by current media selection policies for printed material
- stress that Internet access is a privilege, not a right
- clearly establish the penalties and consequences for abuse of Internet privileges

The Web sites below address these issues as well as others. Samples of AUPs can be viewed and adopted to your specific needs.

Online Permission Slip
http://www.classroom.com/presenters/Campbell1_W98.html

This site contains a sample online permission slip that lists acceptable uses of the Internet as well as good Internet safety.

A Legal and Educational Analysis of K-12 Internet Acceptable Use Policies
http://www.erehwon.com/k12aup/legal_analysis.html

The use of an AUP to govern student and staff behavior raises a number of constitutional concerns. Student and staff constitutional rights must be recognized within the policies.

K-12 Acceptable Use Policies
http://www.erehwon.com/k12aup/

This site contains materials to assist school districts in the development of effective Internet policies and practices.

Houston Independent School District's Acceptable Use Page
http://chico.rice.edu/armadillo/Rice/Resources/acceptable.html

The Texas Studies Gopher began collecting Internet AUP resources a number of years ago. Educators should become familiar with this material before limiting access or establishing policy to minimize the risk of controversy and litigation.

Rice University AUP and Intellectual Freedom Policy Sites
gopher://riceinfo.rice.edu:1170/11/More/Acceptable

Rice University's gopher site contains links to many Acceptable Use Policies and other resources related to ethics, Internet use policies, and censorship.

HOW CAN SCHOOLS BLOCK ACCESS TO OFFENSIVE SITES?

In addition to an AUP, schools can use special software to protect their students and staff from accessing questionable information on the Internet. Exposure to unacceptable Web sites can be prohibited by running monitoring and blocking software designed to disallow access to offensive material.

The following three Web sites link to software that can be used to filter information found on the Internet.

Net Nanny
http://www.netnanny.com

Net Nanny filtering software protects children from questionable material on the Internet. It also can prevent information from going out onto the Internet, such as address, phone number, or other personal and sensitive data.

SurfWatch
http://www.surfwatch.com

SurfWatch offers filtering in five core categories:

- drugs/alcohol/tobacco
- gambling
- hate speech
- sexually explicit
- violence

It also has productivity categories offering a filter in 15 additional areas, including ChatBlock.

WinGuardian
http://www.webroot.com/chap1.htm

This software is for anyone who is concerned with the activities of their computer users, including where the users are going on the Web and what programs they are running. *WinGuardian* can display the acceptable use policy when the system is booted, when a browser is opened, and/or when a screensaver stops. A user must read and click on the AGREE button before they are allowed access to the system.

SUMMARY

The potential for harm to users and the legal liability of school districts are important issues related to the use of the Internet in the K–12 environment. School systems have to justify the worth of their Internet access investment by encouraging productive use of computing resources and discouraging negative or non-productive use of expensive computing and telecommunications systems. A formal policy of use, including consequences of misuse, can help define and monitor Internet access.

Monitoring and blocking software, such as the three listed above, are available to help parents and school systems protect impressionable children and adolescents from the darker sides of the Internet, such as pornography and hate speech.

WHAT DOES RESPONSIBLE ACCESS MEAN?

The Internet has quickly blossomed into a valuable source of information. The value of the information found on the Internet should often be questioned, however. Because the Internet is public domain there are no restrictions on the type of material that can be posted on any Web site. There are no editors or filters for evaluating the information. As a result, information found on the Internet may not always be accurate or credible. *Anyone* can post *anything* on the Internet.

It is the responsibility of the user to evaluate information gathered from the Internet for its accuracy and worth. Responsible users critically read Internet material, acknowledging the subjectivity of any information gathered from the Internet. Teachers and students should follow proper procedures for citing any Internet resources that they may use. As a liable Internet user, these steps are essential to follow to support responsible access.

Guidelines have been developed to help you critically evaluate Web sites but even these guidelines are not yet standardized. To assure that the information you receive from the Internet is valid it may be wise to consider these guidelines along with your own assessment of "good" versus "bad" information. Remember to read with a critical eye. Just because something is in print, doesn't guarantee its accuracy.

Some basic questions to guide your evaluation include:

• Authority
  Who is the author of the piece? What experience do they have? What are their credentials?
• Affiliation
  What organization or institution supports this author? Is this a personal Web site (proceed with caution) or is the material part of an official site?
• Bias
  Is the Web site objective? Does the organization have a political agenda?
• Currency
  When was the information created or last updated? Are the links up-to-date?
• Content
  Are there errors in spelling and grammar? Is the information logical? Does the author include citations or a bibliography when facts or quotations are used?

All information, whether in print or on screen, needs to be critically evaluated by the reader for its credibility and accuracy. These guidelines provide a basic framework for the evaluation of Web-based material. They are by no means complete. For more help on evaluating the credibility and value of Web sites visit the addresses below.

Kathy Schrock's Guide for Educators
http://discoveryschool.com/schrockguide/

This Web site is useful for teachers and students. This site offers ready-made, easy to use Web site evaluation surveys for the elementary, middle, and secondary school levels. It also includes links to other sites on critical evaluation of Internet resources.

Cyberguides
http://www.cyberbee.com/guides.html

This site provides criteria for teachers to use in evaluating content and design of home pages. It also includes ratings sheets for evaluation of content and Web site design.

Blue Web'n
http://www.kn.pacbell.com/wired/bluewebn/rubric.html

Blue Web'n offers an evaluation rubric for assessing the quality of Web pages. It includes key categories and suggestions for scoring.

Southern California College
http://www.sccu.edu/services/Library/www/eval.htm

There are an extensive number of links to Web sites on this site that deal specifically with evaluation of information found on the Internet.

Sites That Discuss Evaluating Web Sites
http://www.lib.mankato.msus.edu/staff/smith/w3evalbm.html

This site includes several links to other sites that address credibility and evaluation of Internet resources.

IF I USE INTERNET MATERIAL, DO I NEED TO CREDIT THE AUTHOR?

Just as with any print material used for research and writing, information gathered from the Internet must be referenced. Proper procedures should be followed for citing all Internet resources including:

- newsgroups
- discussion groups
- Web sites
- electronic journals
- graphics
- online data sources
- all types of articles

Although a number of sites will allow you to use their information without asking permission, an increasing number of authors are requiring permission to use their written work. In this situation a short email message to the author asking for permission to reproduce their work is required. Most authors are more than willing to grant permission. If you have any questions regarding the use of someone's Internet material, it is best to obtain permission as this process requires little time and effort and protects you from any legal concerns.

HOW DO I CITE INFORMATION FROM THE INTERNET?

The purpose of any citation is to lead the reader to all sources used by the writer. Both teachers and students should be aware of the procedures for correctly referencing Internet sources. This is not a simple chore as there are many kinds of materials to be referenced as well as a variety of acceptable citation styles.

Currently, two predominant styles exist for citation of material found on the Internet—The American Psychological Association (APA) and The Modern Language Association (MLA). An example of each follows:

APA style

(A Nonprofit Organization)
National Audubon Society. (1995). A Walk in the Corkscrew Swamp Sanctuary. Available: http://www.audubon.org/audubon/cork.html (visited 1998, November 11)

MLA style

(A Nonprofit Organization)
National Audubon Society. "A Walk in the Corkscrew Swamp Sanctuary," 1995. Online. Available: http://www.audubon.org/audubon/cork.html (11 November 1998)

These examples present only *one* type of Internet resource and are by no means a complete representation of the many different ways to reference Internet materials. Because the user has access to so many kinds of Internet materials it may be wise to visit some of the following sites for a more extensive list of the proper procedures for citing Internet resources.

Citing Electronic Information
http://libweb.sdsu.edu/cite.html

A helpful Web site leading to many links on citation styles and citation of Internet resources.

Tates Creek High School Citing Internet Resources Page
http://www.tatescreek.fayette.k12.ky.us/tchs/Curricul/citing.htm

One high school's home page with links to various Web pages that address procedures for citing Internet resources.

World Wide Words
http://www.quinion.com/words/articles/citation.htm

World Wide Words offers advice on online citation formats. It also provides links to other sites regarding citation styles and procedures.

University of Hartford Libraries and Learning Resources—Citation and Style Guides
http://libaxp.hartford.edu/llr/citestyl.htm

This Web site is another good resource for finding additional Web sites concerned with proper citation of Internet materials.

Bibliographic Format for Citing Electronic Information
http://www.uvm.edu/~ncrane/estyles/

This site includes three general areas—Publication Information, APA Style of Citation, and MLA Style of Citation—with links to additional information on citing Internet resources.

The Internet offers a wealth of information, much of which is neither monitored nor edited. As a result, the user must be responsible for evaluating materials found on the Internet. Internet users should filter material from the Net with questions on its accuracy, value, and quality. Proper citation of Internet sources is also necessary. Users are obligated to give credit to those whose work they use. In short, it is the responsibility of the user to follow appropriate steps and procedures that guarantee responsible access.

SUMMARY

Integrating the Internet into your classroom offers both significant challenges and amazing benefits. If you are just starting to use the Internet you may feel a little anxious about trying to learn all there is to know. However, our advice to you is to simply jump in and get started. The sooner you jump in, the sooner you and your students will benefit from the many resources and learning opportunities offered through the Internet. You may not have, nor may you *ever* have, all the right equipment or all the necessary knowledge; but by opening your door to the possibilities of the Internet, you and your students come one step closer to becoming a WorldWide Classroom.

REFERENCES

Day, K., & Schrum, L. (1995). The Internet and Acceptable Use Policies: What schools need to know. *The ERIC Review, 4*(1), 9–11.
Schrum, L., & Berenfeld, B. (1997). *Teaching and learning in a telecommunications age: A guide to educational telecommunications.* Needham Heights, MA: Allyn and Bacon.

GLOSSARY

Acceptable Use Policy (AUP). An agreement signed by teachers, students, parents, and school administrators that contains a definition of the Internet, a description of use that is acceptable, and a list of steps that will be taken if the Internet is used in an unacceptable manner.

Bookmark. A list of URLs saved within a browser. The user can edit and modify the bookmark list to add and delete URLs as the user's interests change. Bookmark is a term used by Netscape, while Favorites is the term used by Explorer.

Browser. A software program that is used to view and browse information on the Internet.

Bulletin Board Service (BBS). An electronic bulletin board. Information on a BBS is posted to a computer where many can dial in and read it and/or comment on it. BBSs may or may not be connected to the Internet. Some are accessible by modem dial-in only.

Chat mode. A form of online discussion in which messages are exchanged in real time.

Clickable image. An interface used in Web documents that allows the user to click or select different areas of an image (graphic) and link to another Web page or a specific area on the current Web page. Also known as a "hot spot."

Copyright. The exclusive legal right to reproduce, publish, or sell the content of a piece of work.

Database. A file or collection of files that contains records of similar information or data.

Discussion groups. A form of asynchronous electronic communication among several people. Participants connect with others via the Internet to share advice or gather information on topics of interest.

Domain name. The unique name that identifies an Internet site. The naming convention for domain names is two or more parts separated by dots (periods).

Download. The process of transferring a file, document, or program from a remote computer to a local computer. (See also *Upload*)

Email. The short name for electronic mail. Email is sent electronically from one person to another. Emails also can be sent to many different people at the same time by the use of a mailing list.

E-mail address. The location to which an email is addressed. It includes the user ID, the " at" sign (@), the domain name, and an extension.

FAQs (Frequently Asked Questions). A file or document where a moderator or administrator will post commonly asked questions and their answers. If you have a question on any Web site, it is usually best to check for the answer in FAQs first.

Forums. Discussion groups for online participation used to share similar interests or discuss related topics. Forums are messages posted on an electronic bulletin board for anyone to read and respond to.

FTP (File Transfer Protocol). A procedure used to transfer large files and programs from one computer to another. Access to the host computer may or may not require a password.

GIF (Graphics Interchange Format). A format created by CompuServe to allow electronic transfer of digital images.

Home page. A Web document that is the initial or start-up page shown when a Web site is accessed.

HTML (Hypertext Markup Language). The most common language used to write documents that appear as Web pages on the World Wide Web.

HTTP (HyperText Transport Protocol). The common protocol used to communicate between World Wide Web servers.

Hyperlink. Elements within a document (text or graphics) that are used to link to another item or Web page.

Internet. A network of millions of computers that are connected worldwide.

IRC (Internet Relay Chat). A channel is created and users log on to the channel. Anything that is typed is seen by everyone on the channel.

ISP (Internet Service Provider). An organization that provides access to the Internet.

JPEG (Joint Photographic Experts Group). A commonly used graphical file format used to transfer digital images.

Listserv. A mailing list of users who have subscribed. A single email message can be sent at once to the entire list of people.

Mailing list. An electronic list of addresses of users who have subscribed. A mailing list makes it possible to send a single email message to a group of people.

MIDI (Musical Instrument Digital Interface). MIDI files use the .mid file extension. These types of files contain instructions rather than sounds. They are used to transmit information via a digital interface to an FM synthesizer or a wave table device.

MPEG (Motion Picture Experts Group). A format used to make, view, and transfer both digital audio and digital video files

Netiquette (Network Etiquette). Informal guidelines that govern proper behavior on the Internet.

Newsgroups. The name for discussion groups that can be on the Usenet and are established for sharing similar interests or discussing related topics. Newsgroups are messages posted on an electronic bulletin board for anyone to read and respond to.

Plug-in. A program that works within a larger program to add additional capabilities. Plug-ins may have to be downloaded to utilize advanced features of a Web site.

Publishing. The process of uploading Web pages to a Web server.

QuickTime. A format used by Apple Computer to make, view, edit, and send digital audio and video files.

Search engines. Programs on the Internet that categorize information in databases and retrieve that information in the form of searches. Search engines provide two levels of search options: using the categories established by the maintainers of the search engine or conducting keyword searches.

Signature. Information posted on the bottom of a Web page that generally indicates the last date of modification and the party responsible for the maintenance. A signature can also be used at the bottom of an email to identify the sender.

Tag. An HTML command used to mark, or specify the format of, the text that is to be displayed on the Web page.

Telementoring. Web sites with an array of qualified "experts" that can help answer your questions. These experts may be teachers or professionals in the area you are researching. (See also Tutoring)

Telnet. The process of remotely connecting to and using a computer at a distant location.

Tutoring. Web sites that connect a user to "experts" who may provide help by answering questions or assisting on a project. (See also *Telementoring*)

Upload. The process of moving or transferring a document, file, or program from one computer to another computer. (See also *Download*)

URL (Uniform Resource Location). An address used by people on the Internet to locate Web pages. The address includes the protocol used for information transfer, the host computer address, the path to the desired file, and the name of the file requested.

Usenet. A world-wide system of discussion groups. Usenet contains over 10,000 discussion areas, called newsgroups.

Web page. A document that you view in your browser (e.g., Internet Explorer, Netscape). The document can fill one screen or multiple screens, giving the user the ability to scroll to view it all.

WebQuest. An inquiry-oriented activity in which some or all of the information that learners interact with comes from resources on the Internet.

Web server. A software program used to provide, or serve, information to remote computers. Web pages can be "published" to a Web server.

Web site. A group of Web pages that are created and maintained by a group or individuals. Web pages in a Web site generally serve the same purpose.

World Wide Web (WWW). A subset of servers on the Internet that use HTTP to transfer hyperlinked documents in a page-like format.

WorldWide Classroom. A classroom that evolves as educators learn to integrate Internet resources into meaningful curriculum-based learning experiences. A WorldWide Classroom connects teachers and learners to rich resources available through the Internet.

DATE DUE